Teaching Grammar through Writing

Teaching Grammar through Writing

Activities to Develop Writer's Craft in ALL Students in Grades 4-12

Keith Polette

University of Texas, El Paso

PEARSON

Boston   New York   San Francisco
Mexico City   Montreal   Toronto   London   Madrid   Munich   Paris
Hong Kong   Singapore   Tokyo   Cape Town   Sydney

Executive Editor: Aurora Martínez Ramos
Series Editorial Assistant: Lynda Giles
Marketing Manager: Danae April
Production Editor: Paula Carroll
Editorial Production Service: Denise Botelho
Composition Buyer: Linda Cox
Manufacturing Buyer: Linda Moris
Electronic Composition: Schneck-DePippo Graphics
Cover Administrator: Linda Knowles

For related titles and support materials, visit our online catalog at www.ablongman.com.

Between the time website information is gathered and then published, it is not unusual for some sites to have closed. Also, the transcription of URLs can result in typographical errors. The publisher would appreciate notification where these errors occur so that they may be corrected in subsequent editions.

Library of Congress Cataloguing-in-Publication Data
Polette, Keith.
Teaching grammar through writing : activities to develop writer's craft in all students in grades 4–12 / Keith Polette
    p. cm
Includes bibliographical references.
ISBN 0-205-49166-9
1. English language—Grammar—Study and teaching—Activity programs. 2. English language—Composition and exercises—Study and teaching. I. Title.
LB1576.P62 2007
428.2071—dc22   2006052591

Printed in the United States of America

10 9 8 7 6 5 4 3 2 1   11 10 09 08 07

About the Author

Dr. Keith Polette, a specialist in children's literacy, received a Ph.D. in English from Saint Louis University, two Master's Degrees—one in English and one in drama—from Idaho State University, and a B.A. in English from Central Methodist University. Dr. Polette is an Associate Professor of English and the Director of the English Education Program at the University of Texas at El Paso.

Dr. Polette received the UTEP College of Liberal Arts Award for Excellence in Teaching and Research, the UT System Chancellor's Council Award for Excellence in Teaching, and was recognized by the Texas State Reading Association as an Outstanding Texas Author.

Prior to moving to El Paso in 1995, Dr. Polette was a Mentor Teacher and an English/Language Arts teacher for both remedial and gifted students in St. Louis, Missouri.

Dr. Polette has published over thirty articles in professional journals, eight books on teaching, and two books for children. His most recent publications are *Read and Write It Out Loud: Guided Oral Literacy Strategies, Isabel and the Hungry Coyote,* and *Paco and the Giant Chile Plant* (Raven Tree Press).

For the past twenty years, Dr. Polette has given keynote addresses and been a featured speaker at national, regional, and state literacy conferences, and at schools throughout the United States and Canada.

Contents

Chapter 3   *55*

Chapter 4   *74*

Introduction

The structures we use in writing that we rarely use in speech are especially important to understand in a conscious way.

—Martha Kolln, *Rhetorical Grammar: Grammatical Choices, Rhetorical Effects*

When grammar is taught and practiced as a means of communication, rather than as a means for correcting the mechanics and surface accuracy of sentences, it becomes a more purposeful and therefore more motivating focus for classroom learning.

—Martha C. Pennington, *New Ways in Teaching Grammar*

If our rationale for teaching grammar is primarily to improve students' writing, then it would seem that a much more limited and more focused treatment of grammar has a better chance of being effective.

—Constance Weaver, *Teaching Grammar in Context*

Paradoxically, maximizing the benefits of grammar instruction to writing requires teaching less, not more, grammar.

—Rei R. Noguchi, *Grammar and the Teaching of Writing*

Announce, "Today we start our study of grammar," in a typical language arts classroom, and more often than not the students will blanch, roll their eyes, and swoon like you've just unleashed *Beowulf*'s Grendel—that murky creature from the deep who will pounce on them like a monstrous dangling modifier, like a ravenous split infinitive, like a bone-crushing sentence fragment.

Oh grammar, grammar, grammar—how to disarm the Grendel of grammar? Where to begin to tame the beast from the bottom of the bog?

Less Is More

Think of this book as, among other things, a "Grendel-tamer's tool kit" and as a "beginner's guide to grammar wrangling."

Yes, this book is a place *to begin*. It starts with ideas from Weaver and Noguchi: to teach students to subdue the grammar-Grendel, to know the ins and outs of grammar, it is best to teach *less* of it, not more. And it is best to teach grammar in the context of writing, not in isolation.

So this book is tightly focused. Rather than let the grammar-Grendel crash and stomp through the classroom, which is to say, rather than overwhelm students *with too many structures, constructions*, and *rules* (all of which are important in their own right), this book, following Thoreau's dictum to "Simplify, simplify!" asks (and answers) the question: what are the essential elements of grammar that students need to learn to use to become better writers—to become, as we might say in Texas, "right fine grammar wranglers"?

The answer, interestingly enough, comes from written language itself. If we scout the construction of written language, we will discover—eureka!—this: English written language is composed of sixteen elements. And these sixteen elements are the foundational pieces of grammar—the bones of grammar—that students need to learn to use consciously so they can really "rock" their writing, so that can turn Grendels into Beowulfs and bogs into bonds.

Sixteen Elements

So what are these sixteen elements?

They are seven parts of speech, six phrases, and three clauses.

There you have it.

So where do we begin when teaching grammar, when grappling with Grendel? How to we teach our students "less" so that they learn "more"?

We *begin* by teaching students to identify and use the seven parts of speech, six phrases, and three clauses in their writing—in both the prewriting and revision stages of the writing process.

When students learn that writing is first and foremost about words, rather than about "content" or "feelings" or "ideas," they will, paradoxically, find themselves in a stronger position to write about content, feelings, and ideas. In *Image Grammar* Harry Noden writes: "[W]riting is not constructed merely from experiences, information, characters or plots, but from fundamental artistic elements of grammar" (1999, 1). Until students know how to use such "fundamental artistic elements of grammar," their writing will not flourish.

Notice, for instance, this sentence from Walt Whitman's poem "Song of Myself":

> I hear bravuras of birds, bustle of growing wheat, gossip of flames, clack of sticks cooking my meals. (1990, 937)

While, as readers, we may imagine—or hear in our minds—the strong sounds of nature and the crackle and clang of cooking, all we see on the page are words. And while the words enable us to create mental images, the words are just words. What is important about them is that they are skillfully, grammatically arranged to evoke images and associations within us. In other words, the words are, as Noden says, "artistic."

If we look at Whitman's sentence from a grammatical and analytical point of view, we see that it contains vivid, concrete nouns and verbs. It has a clear subject and predicate, and it deftly employs, as direct objects, four nouns plus four prepositional phrases and one participial phrase. In other words, it has a clear and discernible grammatical structure.

One of the most powerful ways to enable students to develop the skills necessary to write effectively is to teach grammar within the context of writing. When students first learn the tools of writing and grammar-wrangling—the seven parts of speech, six phrases, and three clauses—and then consciously and deliberately use them in their writing repeatedly (especially in the drafting and revision stages of the writing process), they will undergo transformations from being uninformed (and often struggling) writers to becoming more informed, independent, and reflective writers. Which is to say that for students to be able to conjure and craft such sentences as Whitman's they must be able to know and use the sixteen "fundamental artistic elements of grammar." In this way students will remove the monster mask from the face of Grendel and falter in front of him no more.

The Benefits of Teaching Grammar through Writing

- **To meet national standards.** The IRA/NCTE language arts standard number 6 encourages students "to apply knowledge of language structure and language conventions" in their writing. One way to meet this standard is to teach students how to use grammatical structures—phrases and clauses—purposefully in their writing. When students learn to use such structures deliberately, they will necessarily develop and apply their knowledge of "language structure and language conventions" to their own writing (Haussamen, Benjamin, Kolln, and Wheeler 2003).

- **To provide student writers with useful tools.** When students discover that there are sixteen basic tools for writing (seven parts of speech, six phrases, three clauses), they will realize that such tools are easy to assimilate—if these tools are taught in a sequential, nonthreatening, student-centered way. Once students learn what these writer's tools are and how to use them, they will find that they have more choices as writers than they previously had. Rather than rely on their internal—

and unconscious—language schema for writing purposes, students will begin to make choices about how they will construct the sentences that form—and inform—whatever writing form (genre) they are crafting (Good 2002; Kolln 1999; Noden 1999).

■ **To enable students to develop a sense of voice.** As students learn to use the writer's tools, they will free themselves from a one-voice approach to writing and will move toward the ability to use different voices for different purposes. Because "voice" derives from the arrangement of grammatical elements in writing (words, phrases, and clauses), when students learn to manipulate these elements, they will learn to strengthen, modify, and change their voice in writing. And from the ability to choose the appropriate voice in writing comes a sense of personal agency and power (Weaver 1996).

■ **To show students that the use of grammar is part of a process, not an end in itself.** When students use grammatical elements—especially in the revision and editing stages—as part of the writing process, they will see how the use of grammar affords them clear choices—choices that, in the past, they may have never been aware of. Once students have learned to use grammatical elements, they can approach the revising stage from a freshly informed perspective; they can, for instance, decide to change, add, or delete a word, phrase, or clause rather than merely think about altering the content of their writing. Such an approach is essential in helping students see that, for the most part, their writing is and should be "reader-focused." That is, students must learn that when they write for an audience other than themselves, they need to employ those grammatical tools that will help their readers clearly understand what has been written (Noden 1999; Weaver 1996; Hudson 1992).

■ **To help students become critical thinkers.** When students use grammar in their writing, they must learn to make careful decisions not only about which words, phrases, and clauses to use, but why. In other words, to write effectively, students must know what effects can be achieved by using various combinations of words, phrases, and clauses, and they must adjust these effects to fit the content, purpose(s), and audiences for their writing. When students begin to make such adjustments in a deliberate manner, they are exercising the dynamics of critical thinking (Calderonello, Martin, and Blair 2003; Thurman 2002; Kolln 1999; Noden 1999).

- **To enable students to develop confidence as writers.** By knowing what tools to use and how (and when and why) to use them, students will develop confidence as writers. Just as a carpenter must know which tools and materials to use to achieve his or her ends, so, too, must writers. If a carpenter were to build a chair that needed to be strong enough to support a great deal of weight, she would probably not choose spruce; and she would not simply glue the wood together or the construction would be a disaster and would not achieve its purpose. Similarly, writers must make careful choices. When students know how to make the choices that best suit their writing purposes, their self-confidence will grow (Haussamen, Benjamin, Kolln, and Wheeler 2003).

- **To help English language learners develop a working knowledge of the conventions of English.** When grammar is taught as a means of communication and construction, English language learners (ELLs) will become more proficient in using the conventions of English for genuine purposes. Moreover, by learning how to use writer's tools, ELL students will make gains in their understanding of English (Pennington 1995).

No one writes a perfect draft at the first sitting. Writing well is a messy business; it takes time, thought, reflection, and rewriting. During the rewriting stage, authors may add, delete, or change words; they may add, delete, or change phrases and clauses; and they may rearrange entire sentences, stanzas, or paragraphs. Many young writers, however, think of writing as filling space, as completing an assignment, not as a recursive process that requires a good deal of attention and concentration. Because many young writers do not know what kinds of choices they have—what kinds of grammatical tools to use—they usually want to get their writing done as swiftly as they can.

Ideas to Promote Grammatical Awareness

- **Read aloud.** When we read aloud to our students every day, we enable them to hear "artistic" arrangements of words and sentences. After a time, students will begin to assimilate those arrangements and use them in their own writing. Remember: if students have not internalized words and language structures, they cannot use them in their writing. (For more information about this topic, see my book *Read and Write It Out Loud: Guided Oral Literacy Strategies* published by Allyn & Bacon.)

- **Minilessons.** Using minilessons gives students just enough information they need; it does not overwhelm them. Minilessons are also just long enough to help students learn new content. Students then use the material presented in the minilessons in their writing.

- **Writer's notebook.** It is essential that students keep a writer's notebook. In these notebooks, students record new words, phrases, and sentences. Students also jot down notable words and phrases from books they are reading.

- **Scaffolding.** Students need to be guided through lots of writing activities if they are to improve as writers. By guiding students through the writing process—prewriting, drafting, revising, editing/sharing—teachers can help students stay focused, not become lost, and make critical decisions about their own writing.

- **Conferencing.** Students benefit greatly from conferencing with their teacher. As students write, the teacher may wish to conference with them, both formally and informally, to assess and help them with their writing.

How to Use This Book

The book can be used sequentially. It begins with ideas about and writing activities for parts of speech, phrases, and clauses, followed by chapters on punctuation, kinds of sentences, and voice. The book concludes with sixteen process-writing activities that invite students to use all they have learned about grammar in their own writing.

The book can be used as it is arranged, or it can be used as the teacher needs to use it. If the teacher sees that she needs to spend time first, for example, on phrases, the book will easily lend itself to that use. Moreover, the teacher may or may not use all of the writing activities; he may use these as springboards to the creation of his own. Finally, the teacher can modify the activities to tailor them to students' needs.

The teacher will notice that the writing activities at the end of the book are based on poetry rather than on paragraphs, essays, stories, and so on. The reason for this is twofold.

First, many, if not most, students see writing as the "filling of space" rather than the conscious and judicious use of sharply defined strategies to construct a form that conveys clear content to a specific audience for a pointed purpose (or purposes). Which is to say that when students are asked to write, they often ask this question: "How long should the writing be?" When students write "to fill space," their writing will usually be unorganized, incoherent, and unfocused. When students are asked to write poetry—and are given clear and effective procedures for doing so—they will not be put off by the length of what they are asked to write. Because the poems are fairly short, they will not be intimidating or daunting forms for students to construct.

Second, the focus of this book is to teach students to use grammatical elements in their writing. Since the poems are short and structurally uncomplicated, students will find more success in using grammatical elements. By writing the poems that are articulated in this book, students will not get lost or bogged down by trying to craft forms that are complicated and overwhelming. After students learn to use grammatical elements via the crafting of poetry, they may *transfer* those elements to more complicated forms (paragraphs, essays, and stories). Remember: the goal is to teach students first how to use the sixteen grammatical elements in their writing. And by teaching students to construct and revise poems that do not have overly complicated structures, we will not overwhelm them; rather, we will enable them to develop the skills and confidence they need to become more conscious and more effective writers. In other words, let's ask students to learn one thing at a time—first things first. Let's not ask too much of them; let's, instead, guide them to write in ways that are clear so that they can learn, expand, and transfer the skills they learn.

A Final Note

This book is neither designed, nor intended, to be a traditional, "comprehensive" book of grammar instruction—*because the traditional approach to teaching grammar fails to improve students' writing abilities.* Rather, this book is a place *to begin.* As such, it does not contain the plethora of grammatical and usage elements found in traditional, large grammar tomes. Additionally, this book does not focus on theories of grammar or on different conceptions of grammar. Rather, this book assumes a more modest and a more pragmatic approach. It is designed to teach students to learn to recognize, and then consciously use in their writing, sixteen essential grammatical elements: seven parts of speech, six phrases, and three clauses. When students shift their emphasis from being content driven in their writing to making conscious choices about the manner in which they convey that content (i.e., by choosing to use and combine the sixteen grammatical elements), they will have made substantial growth as writers.

Teaching Grammar through Writing

Word Works I

1. **What do these words have in common?**

boy	girl	man	woman
teacher	student	principal	cook
brother	sister	cousin	uncle
acrobat	nurse	lawyer	clown

2. **What do these words have in common?**

swamp	beach	street	city
St. Louis	El Paso	Denver	Boise
United States	Ireland	Missouri	Tibet
New Zealand	Idaho	Montana	Oregon

3. **What do these words have in common?**

house	fence	grass	door
mirror	lamp	toothbrush	watch
soap	dish	book	desk
shoe	pencil	bucket	telephone

4. **What do these words have in common?**

happiness	sadness	fear	anger
truth	justice	honesty	beauty
pride	loyalty	love	hate
jealousy	envy	courage	peace

5. **What do all the words in activities 1, 2, 3, and 4 have in common?**

Answer to Activity 5: All the words are NOUNS.

■ What is a noun?

■ Tell what you think a noun is: _____

A NOUN is a word that names a PERSON, a PLACE, or a THING.
Nouns can name things that we can touch, taste, see, hear, feel, and smell.
These are called CONCRETE NOUNS.

Activity 1 is a list of nouns that name different kinds of PEOPLE.
Activity 2 is a list of nouns that name different kinds of PLACES.
Activity 3 is a list of nouns that name different kinds of THINGS.

Nouns also name things we cannot touch, taste, see, hear, feel, or smell. These are called ABSTRACT NOUNS.

Activity 4 is a list of nouns that names different kinds of EMOTIONS and IDEAS. Words that name emotions and ideas are ABSTRACT NOUNS.

■ Think of five more nouns that name different people: _____

■ Think of five more nouns that name different places: _____

■ Think of five more nouns that name different things: _____

■ Think of five more nouns that name different emotions and ideas (abstract nouns):

_____

Writing Activity I: Nouns

Complete the following pattern with abstract and concrete nouns. In the first blank put an abstract noun; in the second blank put a concrete noun that tells something about the abstract noun.

I can't see _____ , but I can see _____ .

I can't see <u>love</u>, but I can see a <u>wedding ring</u>.

I can't see <u>chaos</u>, but I can see a <u>tornado</u>.

I can't see <u>happiness</u>, but I can see a <u>smile</u>.

I can't hear <u>anger</u>, but I can hear a <u>yelling</u>.

I can't hear <u>peace</u>, but I can hear a <u>silence</u>.

I can't see <u>joy</u>, but I can see _____ .

I can't hear <u>sadness</u>, but I can hear _____ .

I can't hear <u>victory</u>, but I can hear _____ .

I can't see <u>innocence</u>, but I can see _____ .

I can't see <u>peace</u>, but I can see _____ .

I can't see <u>beauty</u>, but I can see _____ .

I can't see _____ , but I can see _____ .

I can't hear _____ , but I can hear _____ .

Writing Activity II: *Nouns*

Complete the following pattern with concrete nouns. In the blank put a concrete noun that is an example of the underlined abstract noun.

If _____ were an animal, it would be a _____.

If <u>anger</u> were an animal, it would be a <u>tiger</u>.

If <u>anger</u> were an animal, it would be a _____.

If <u>fear</u> were an animal, it would be a _____.

If <u>playfulness</u> were an animal, it would be a _____.

If <u>loyalty</u> were an animal, it would be a _____.

If <u>beauty</u> were an animal, it would be a _____.

If <u>boredom</u> were an animal, it would be a _____.

If <u>speed</u> were an animal, it would be a _____.

If <u>determination</u> were an animal, it would be a _____.

If <u>bravery</u> were an animal, it would be a _____.

If <u>loneliness</u> were an animal, it would be a _____.

Writing Activity III: *Nouns*

Complete the following pattern with an abstract noun and an -ing phrase.

Use this pattern: _____ is _____.

In the first blank, put an abstract noun. In the second blank put an -ing phrase that tells something specific about the abstract noun.

Fear is going into the basement alone at night.

Fear is seeing a pit bull charging you.

Fear is singing a song to a room of strangers.

Fear is admitting that you broke the window.

Try your own.

6. **What do these words have in common?:**

   animal   country   game   food
   movie   book   group   building
   plant   city   person

7. **What do these words have in common?**

bullfrog	oak tree	*Star Wars*	George Washington
Seattle	Chicago	Monopoly	Empire State Building
tacos	the Beatles	Australia	*Where the Wild Things Are*

Answer to Activity 6: These words are GENERAL NOUNS.
Answer to Activity 7: These words are SPECIFIC NOUNS.

CONCRETE NOUNS—nouns that are names for people, places, and things that you can touch, taste, see, hear, feel, and smell—also come in two flavors: GENERAL and SPECIFIC.

General nouns are words that name different groups of things.
Specific nouns are words that name different particular things.

animal is a general noun.   *person* is a general noun.
bullfrog is a specific noun.   *George Washington* is a specific noun.

city is a general noun.   *movie* is a general noun.
Seattle is a specific noun.   *Star Wars* is a specific noun.

country is a general noun.
Australia is a specific noun.

■ Think of two SPECIFIC NOUNS for each GENERAL NOUN:

EXAMPLE:

General	Specific
music	rock 'n' roll, jazz
bird	owl, hummingbird
dog	collie, Chihuahua
expression	frown, grin

city   _____

country   _____

book   _____

person   _____

weather   _____

expression _____

clothing   _____

game   _____

plant   _____

author   _____

General Nouns Contain Lots of Specific Nouns

Think of a few general nouns: *baseball*, *winter*, *summer*, *birthday*, *storm*, etc. Choose one and think of specific nouns that combine to make the general noun. Use this pattern:
_____ is: _____ .

EXAMPLE:

Summer is: ice cream, sunburns, swimming pools, T-shirts, shorts, and bicycles.

There are two other kinds of nouns: *proper nouns* and *common nouns*. Proper nouns are capitalized; commons nouns are not.

We capitalize nouns when

■ They refer to specific people: Tom, Mary, the Smiths, Dr. Einstein, Mr. Jones, Mrs. Caldwell, Uncle James, Aunt Eloise, William Shakespeare.

■ They refer to days of the week, months, and holidays: Sunday, Tuesday, July, Christmas.

■ They refer to specific places that have names: Miami, Tennessee, the Missouri River, the Pacific Ocean, Main Street, the Teton Mountains, the Washington Monument, Franklin State Park, Sweden, Italy.

■ They refer to people from other countries: Germans, Japanese, Italians, Tibetans, Americans.

■ They refer to periods in history: the Revolutionary War, the War of 1812, the Victorian Era.

■ They refer to titles of books, plays, articles, or movies (articles and prepositions are usually not capitalized): *Where the Wild Things Are, The Wind in the Willows, Hamlet,* "Reading Books Is Good for Your Brain," *Star Wars.*

■ They refer to specific teams or organizations: the St. Louis Cardinals, the Green Party, the National Council of Teachers of English.

■ They refer to schools or businesses: the University of Texas at El Paso, Apple Computer, Smith Elementary School.

■ They refer to regions of the United States: Southwest, Midwest, Northeast.

Writing Activity IV: *Nouns*

Step One
Think of three concrete "people" nouns:

_____

Think of three concrete "place" nouns:

_____

Think of three concrete "thing" nouns:

_____

Think of three abstract nouns:

_____

Step Two
From each of the four kinds of nouns you have written, choose one—that will be a total of four nouns: one people noun, one place noun, one thing noun, and one abstract noun.

Step Three
Use all four nouns in one sentence. The sentence must make sense.

The Right Words

Using the right words makes writing zing with life; the right words create clear ideas and concrete images. Usually the right words are ones that are specific, not general, concrete, not abstract. To begin to find the right words try the following techniques.

Found Nouns

In a writer's notebook, keep a record of interesting, vivid, or unusual nouns. Look for these kinds of nouns in stories, books, magazines, and poems. Try to find at least ten nouns per week. Here's an example:

albatross	villain	blimp
zephyr	victrola	parchment
tome	fiord	current
maze	carrion	festival
fragment	dungeon	swamp
meadow	creek	laser

Can you add more vivid nouns?

_____   _____   _____

_____   _____   _____

Word Walls

Make a word wall by making a list of specific nouns that belong under the category of a general noun. Try to add a few nouns each week. A word wall may take three to four weeks to complete. The words on the word wall are a great source for spelling and writing activities. Here's a sample list:

Folktale Nouns

apple	ashes	basket
briars	bricks	bridge
cape	castle	crumbs
dwarf	elf	forest
frog	giant	hen
king	lantern	mirror
moat	slipper	straw
sticks	troll	wolf

_____   _____   _____

_____   _____   _____

Can you think of specific nouns for these categories?

summer nouns, winter nouns, autumn nouns, spring nouns, baseball nouns, story nouns, science fiction nouns, movie nouns, school nouns, song nouns, ocean nouns, city nouns

Replacement Nouns
Replace the general nouns in the following with specific nouns.

EXAMPLE:

I'm no turtle,
but I carry a sack on my back—
for in my sack are all my things.
[drop "all my things" and add specific things that might be in the sack].

Now you try:
The machine hummed as the animal jumped after the insect.
The guy climbed up the big plant.

Dwindle Down with Nouns
Think of some general nouns. Choose one. Think of nouns that become less and less general until you end with a specific noun + an -ing phrase or two. For example:

animal—bird—owl—Great Horned Owl gliding through a shadowy forest, searching for movement

animal—amphibian—frog—red-eyed tree frog clutching a tiny tree limb, holding its breath, waiting for a circling hawk to glide away

Try your own:

Word Works II

1. **What do these words have in common?**

pour	run	skip	drink
laugh	toss	sent	open
soar	catch	swim	carry

2. **What do these words have in common?**

am	are	is	was
were	will be	have been	will have been

   Answer to Activities 1 and 2: The words are all VERBS.

■ What is a verb?

■ Tell what you think a verb is: _____

VERBS are words that refer to ACTIONS or STATES OF BEING.

All the words in Activity 1 show action. Action verbs often are followed in a sentence by a direct object or an indirect object. For example, in the sentence, Snow White bit the apple, "apple" is the direct object of the verb "bit." Here's another example: The witch cut Rapunzel's hair. "Rapunzel's hair" is the direct object of the verb "cut."

Here are sentences that contain indirect objects. An indirect object is often a noun or pronoun that comes before the direct object. The indirect object usually tells to whom or for whom the action of the verb is happening.

The witch gave Snow White the apple.
("Snow White" is the indirect object of the verb "gave"; "apple" is the direct object.)

The apple caused her much grief.
("Her" is the indirect object; "grief" is the direct object.)

The troll offered the giant a harp.
("Giant" is the indirect object; "harp" is the direct object.)

All the words in Activity 2 show states of being; these verbs do not show actions. These verbs "link" the subject in the sentence to a word (or words) that give information (a description) about it.

VERBS appear in six different forms, or tenses:

PRESENT TENSE: The frog jumps.
PAST TENSE: The frog jumped.
FUTURE TENSE: The frog will jump.
PRESENT PERFECT TENSE: The frog has jumped six times today.
PAST PERFECT TENSE: The frog had jumped only once before it rained.
FUTURE PERFECT TENSE: The frog will have jumped more than one hundred times by next Sunday.

3. **What differences do you see between the sentences in column 1 and those in column 2?**

The boy hit the ball.	The ball was hit.
The dog ate the food.	The food was eaten.
The girl popped the balloon.	The balloon was popped.
The woman rang the doorbell.	The doorbell was rung.
The singer sang the song.	The song was sung.
The teacher read the book.	The book was read.
The firemen put out the fire.	The fire was put out.

Answer to Activity 3: The sentences in column 1 are written in ACTIVE VOICE. The sentences in column 2 are written in PASSIVE VOICE.

In the ACTIVE VOICE, the subject of the sentence—the person, animal, or thing performing the action—is present *before* the verb.

In the PASSIVE VOICE, the subject of the sentence is usually not present. If the subject of the sentence is present it is often at the end of a prepositional phrase (it is the object of a preposition). For example, in the sentence, The book was eaten by the troll, the subject "troll" is the object of the preposition "by."

Writing Activity: Verbs

Change the following sentences from PASSIVE VOICE to ACTIVE VOICE. You may need to add a subject to some of the sentences.

EXAMPLES:

The man was bitten by a mosquito. (passive voice)
The mosquito bit the man. (active voice)

The shed was burned by the fire. (passive voice)
The fire burned the shed. (active voice)

Now try your own:

The movie was watched by the whole family.

_____

The computer was turned on by the student.

_____

The giant was fooled by Jack.

_____

The princess was put to sleep by the magic apple.

_____

The bridge was crossed by the three billy goats.

_____

The straw was spun into thread.

_____

The gold was touched.

_____

The golden egg was laid.

_____

Many writers agree that VERBS are the most important words in sentences. Verbs fill sentences with horsepower and make the words dash across the page. The right verb can turn a dull sentence into one that gallops.

4. **What differences do you notice between the verbs in column 1 and those in column 2?**

ran	scampered
said	exclaimed
held	gripped
went	scurried
walked	moseyed
saw	spied
opened	ripped
cut	hacked
fell	tumbled
attached	stitched
showed	unfurled
closed	slammed
turned	whirled
ate	devoured
separate	split
took	seized

Answer to Activity 4: The verbs in column 2 are more specific and more vivid than the verbs in column 1.

■ Replace the weak verbs in the following sentences with ones that are more specific and vivid.

EXAMPLES:

He went down the street.
He *sauntered* down the street.

She cut down the tree with the axe.
She *hacked* down the tree with the axe.

Now try your own:

The giant went after Jack.

_____

Jack went down the beanstalk.

_____

The goat pushed the troll off the bridge.

_____

King Midas held the gold coin.

_____

Cinderella cleaned the stove.

_____

Word Walls

Make a word wall by making a list of specific verbs that belong under the category of a general noun. Try to add a few verbs each week. Here's an example:

Folktale Verbs

devoured	agonized	clamored	climbed	clutched	dashed
gazed	grazed	journeyed	growled	plodded	raced
scampered	shivered	stole	sunk	tromped	whined

■ Can you think of specific verbs for these categories?
summer verbs, winter verbs, autumn verbs, spring verbs, baseball verbs, story verbs, science fiction verbs, movie verbs, school verbs, song verbs, ocean verbs, city verbs, verbs for the word *walk,* verbs for the word *see,* verbs for the word *move*

■ Think of specific verbs for more general verbs: write, eat, run, call, etc.

EXAMPLES:

Write: print, scribble, scrawl, jot, note, scratch, draft
Run: dash, scamper, scoot, scurry, shin, sprint, career, course, race, bustle, hurry, hustle, rush, flit, fly, hasten, highball, hotfoot, hustle, rush, bolt, book

Try your own:

What Am I?

Think of a specific noun (animal or machine); think of four or five specific actions that the animal or machine does. Use this pattern:

I _____ , and I _____ , and I _____ ,

and I _____ . What am I?

EXAMPLES:

I leap, and I plop, and I swim, and I croak. What am I? (A frog!)
I flit, and I fly, I flutter, and I fold my wings. What am I? (A butterfly!)

Try your own:

Three Verb Combinations

Think of an animal, an object, or a machine; think of three actions that the animal, object, or machine does. Tell where the animal or machine does each action.

EXAMPLES:

The mighty bullfrog swims through the pond, leaps to a lily pad, and croaks beneath the moon.
The comet soared through the skies, arced from star to star, and raced around the sun.

Try your own:

Writing Activity I: *Replacement Words*

Replace weak verbs with vivid verbs and general nouns with specific nouns.

EXAMPLES:

When I got to the place, I heard the people talking.
I got some stuff and sat down to watch the things were up in the air.

When I moseyed into the park, I heard children chattering.
I bought a bag of popcorn and plopped down to watch fireworks exploding in the air.

Try replacing the weak verbs and general nouns in this one:

The animal went into the place.

Other animals above it made noise.

Some other animals went away.

And other animals went into the air.

Writing Activity II: *A Sound-List Poem*

Step One
Think of six different animals. Be specific. Rather than write "dog," write "a German Shepherd." Rather than write "bird," write "a blue jay."

Think of words—verbs—for the noises that the animals make. Be specific. Rather than write "sings" for blue jay, write "screeches."

Think of six different things that make noise in the city. Be specific. Rather than write "car," write "a taxi cab." Rather than write "truck," write "garbage truck."

Think of words—verbs—for the noises that the things in the city make. Be specific. Rather than write "makes noise" for taxi cab, write "honks."

Step Two

Put your animals and the sounds they make in one stanza; put the things from the city and the noises they make in another stanza.

Begin and end stanza one with this line:
Noisy animals, noisy animals everywhere.

Begin and end stanza two with this line:
City noise, city noise fills the air.

Step Three

Create your poem. Here's an example.

> Noisy animals, noisy animals everywhere.
> Hummingbirds whirr.
> Bullfrogs groan.
> Hawks screech.
> Moths flutter.
> Chihuahuas yap.
> Tigers snarl.
> Noisy animals, noisy animals everywhere.
>
> City noise, city noise fills the air.
> Jackhammers chatter.
> Tires squeal.
> Sirens wail.
> Crowds roar.
> Moving trucks moan.
> Trains hiss.
> City noise, city noise fills the air.

■ Try writing another sound-list poem about fairy-tale characters: dwarfs, trolls, giants, ogres, elves, wolves, children, frogs, kings, queens, princesses, princes. Use a specific action verb to tell what each one does.

Words Work in Different Ways

Can you tell what these words have in common?

cake	star	change	place	bank
clown	curve	yoke	fall	arc
bend	plot	sink	play	share

These words are *multiple-meaning words*. They can be used as either nouns or verbs in sentences (and some can be used as adjectives).

The gremlin's favorite food was pumpkin cake.
The gremlin had food caked on his face.

When Jack came to a bend in the road, he didn't know which way to go.
The giant had to bend the beanstalk in half before he could yank it out of the ground.

■ Choose three words from the list and use them in one sentence.

■ Use the same three words in another sentence, but don't use them the same way.

Word Works III

1. Tell what these words have in common:

I	me	you	he
she	we	us	they
them	it	this	that
my	your	her	his
its	our	their	who

Answer to Activity 1: The words are all PRONOUNS.

■ What is a pronoun?

■ Tell what you think a pronoun is: _____

A PRONOUN is a word that takes the place of a noun. A PRONOUN is a stand-in for a noun.

PRONOUNS come in three flavors, or cases: subjective, objective, and possessive. Subjective pronouns appear as "subjects" of sentences and phrases. Objective pronouns appear as "objects" of sentences, phrases, and clauses. Possessive pronouns show ownership of a noun.

Subjective Case	Objective Case	Possessive Case
I read.	Read to me.	my book
You read.	Joan reads to you.	your book
She reads.	Read to her.	her book
He reads.	Read to him.	his book
It reads.	Read to it.	its book
We read.	Read to us.	our book
They read.	Read to them.	their book
Who reads?	To whom does she read?	

This is a great book.	Give this to me.
That is a lousy book.	Give that to her.

There are also different kinds of pronouns:

Reflexive Pronouns refer to themselves: myself, yourself, himself, herself, itself, ourselves, yourselves, themselves

Demonstrative Pronouns indicate specific persons, places, or things: this, that, these, those.

Indefinite Pronouns point to, generally not specifically, persons, places, or things: all, any, anyone, both, either, everybody, everyone, few, many, most, neither, nobody, none, several, some, somebody, someone

Relative Pronouns introduce clauses: which, who, whom, whose, that

Interrogative Pronouns introduce questions: what, which, who, whom, whose

■ Use pronouns in the right case when using them in a sentence.

The queen gave the medals to Cinderella and I. (incorrect because "I" is a subjective pronoun that is used as the object of a preposition)
The queen gave the medals to Cinderella and me. (correct)

Her and me hiked to the castle to get our medals. (incorrect because "her and me" are objective pronouns used as a compound subject)
She and I hiked to the castle to get our medals. (correct)

Us are the best elves in the enchanted forest. (incorrect because "us" is an objective pronoun used as part of a compound subject)
We are the best elves in the enchanted forest. (correct)

The giant is taller than me. (incorrect because "me" is an objective pronoun used as an adjective)
The giant is taller than I. (correct)

Him and her are the fastest frogs. (incorrect because "him and her" are objective pronouns used as compound subjects)
He and she are the fastest frogs. (correct)

Them are shiny apples. (incorrect because "them" is an objective pronoun used as a subject)
They are shiny apples. (correct)

Him and I crossed the bridge. (incorrect because "him" is an objective pronoun used as a subject)
He and I crossed the bridge. (correct)

It was me who found the apple. (incorrect because "me" is an objective pronoun used as a predicate nominative)
It was I who found the apple. (correct)

It was him spinning straw into golden thread. (incorrect because "him" is an objective pronoun used as a predicate nominative)
It was he spinning straw into golden thread. (correct)

It was them who helped Snow White. (incorrect because "them" is an objective pronoun used as a predicate nominative)
It was they who helped Snow White. (correct)

That's her who fell asleep. (incorrect because "her" is an objective pronoun used as a predicate nominative)
That's she who fell asleep. (correct)

■ Use each set of pronouns in different sentences.

I and he	she and her
we and they	him and her
mine and theirs	who and whose

■ Remember: If you use subjective pronouns, begin a sentence with:

She and I
He and I
They and I
The giant and I
Cinderella, Rapunzel, and I

■ If you use pronouns after linking verbs (is, are, was, etc.), they must be subjective pronouns.

It was I who
It was he who
It was she who
It was they who
It is he who
It is she who

Word Works IV

1. **What do these words have in common?**

dim	moldy	wrinkled	smooth
shiny	sharp	cracked	fuzzy
spotted	frozen	hazy	slick
muted	sour	sweet	spicy

2. **What do these words have in common?**

beautiful	ugly	sad	anxious
pretty	nice	mean	democratic
fair	bad	good	boring

Answer to Activities 1 and 2: The words are all ADJECTIVES.

■ What is an adjective?

■ Tell what you think an adjective is: _____

Answer: ADJECTIVES are words that describe—give more information about—nouns and pronouns.

Adjectives tell *which*: this frog, that giant, those dwarfs.
Adjectives tell *what kind*: the green frog, the lonely giant, the frozen lake.
Adjective also tell *how many*: many frogs, several giants, one lake, seven dwarfs.
Adjectives can also work together: this green frog, that lonely giant, those seven dwarfs.

All the words in Activity 1 are *concrete* adjectives. These adjectives give information that we can see, touch, taste, hear, and smell.

All the words in Activity 2 are *abstract* adjectives. They do not give information about what we can see, touch, taste, hear, or smell. They give an idea about something. For example, *the bad troll* tells us that the person who wrote the sentence thinks the troll is *bad*; it does not tell us what the troll looks like. *The green troll* tells us something about how the troll looks: he is *green*.

Too Many Adjectives

Adjectives can help make writing clearer and more specific. But adjectives should usually be used sparingly. Too many adjectives will spoil the sentence! For example, this sentence has too many adjectives:

"We went into the big, old dark, cold, scary, empty, rotten house." The adjectives in this sentence do not create a picture; instead they tell the reader what to think about the room, not what to see.

Here's a better sentence, one that uses just a few adjectives:

"We stepped into the house. We saw wrinkled wallpaper, shattered windows, and a gaping hole where the staircase used to be." The second sentence shows that the house was old and falling apart; it does not tell the reader what to think or how to feel.

Remember: As a general rule, use adjectives that show, not ones that tell.

Word Wall

Make a word wall of adjectives that describe the same general thing:

Fairy-tale characters, summer, winter, school, birthdays, holidays, animals, games, friends, family, picnics, vacations, etc.

■ Replace the weak adjectives in the following sentences with ones that are more specific and vivid.

EXAMPLE:
We saw the pretty lake.
We saw the *shimmering* lake.

Snow White bit the bad apple.

_____

Jack hacked down the ugly beanstalk.

_____

The goat sniffed the uneatable grass.

_____

The princess gazed at the beautiful sunset.

_____

Writing Activity I: *Alliterative Adjectives*

Some writers use adjectives in a special way. They put two or three of them together, and these adjectives all begin with the same sound. These are called alliterative adjectives.

Here's an example from Edgar Allen Poe: "During the whole of a dull, dark, and soundless day...." Notice all the *D* sounds.

Here are some other examples:

The curious, curved caterpillar crept across the cracked branch.
The determined, dotted Dalmatian dragged the dizzy fireman to safety.
The groaning, grumpy giant grabbed the sack of golden eggs.
The tired, toothless troll tugged at the ropes of his tattered tent.

Write two sentences that have alliterative adjectives.

Writing Activity II: *Replacing Words That Tell with Words That Show*

Adjectives cannot act alone. They have to work with other words, especially with nouns and verbs. If writing is going to be clear and specific, all three kinds of words need to work together like a team.

Here's an example of how adjectives, nouns, and verbs do not work together to create clear and specific pictures in writing. They are too general.

My room is a real mess. There's stuff everywhere. Things are all over the place. It doesn't even look like my room.

This description only tells the reader that the room is a "mess"; it does not describe the things in the room; it doesn't paint a clear picture with words.

Here's what happens when the general adjectives, nouns, and verbs are replaced with more concrete and specific ones.

My room looks like a tornado hit it. Strewn on the floor are heaps and bundles of clothes. Crumpled and crinkled papers and torn and tattered candy wrappers litter the desk. Faded, dingy curtains hang like flags at half-mast; behind them a mud-splattered window filters the sun in blotches. The doors of the closet hang at deranged angles; inside, shoes and sweaters lay in piles beneath bent and twisted hangers.

This description is better because it lets the reader see that the room is a "mess," but it doesn't tell the reader directly.

■ Try creating a description of something you know.

Step One: Getting Started
Brainstorm a list of things you might be able to describe. Don't try to describe something too big.

Examples: a pet, a room, a favorite place, an animal, a character from a story, and so on. Pick one thing to describe. Make a list of concrete details about the thing you have chosen.

EXAMPLE:

An animal: dragon

List of details:

 body as large as a two-story building
 body covered with sharp, green scales
 arms as thick as telephone poles
 claws on the feet and hands
 head the size of an SUV
 mouth filled with rows of deadly teeth
 fiery eyes

Step Two: Drafting

Put your ideas together in a draft, a sloppy copy. Begin by describing your subject either from top to bottom, bottom to top, right to left, or left to right. Also start your description with a sentence that lets the reader know what you are going to describe and what the general idea is. For example, "The dragon was a frightening creature." The word *frightening* lets the reader know what idea you will create in your description.

Here's a way to begin a draft:

The _____ was _____ .

The meadow was beautiful.   The dungeon was horrible.
The eagle was majestic.   The ogre was ugly.

Write a draft of the description, like this:

> The dragon was a frightening creature. It stood up. It was taller than a two-story building. The dragon spread its wings. It opened its mouth, which had rows of deadly teeth. It spit fire. Its red eyes flashed. The dragon flew away.

Step Three: Revising Look at the Draft

Now try to replace any weak adjectives, nouns, and verbs with stronger ones. Also try to use some alliteration:

> The dragon was a frightening creature. It roared and reared, whipping its slithering, slimy-scaled body to its full height. Taller than a two-story building, the dragon spread its wide wings and beat the air with thunderous blasts and bursts. It opened its mouth, which was lined with rows of jagged teeth, and spewed a searing stream of fire. As its laser-red eyes flashed at something in the distance, the dragon launched itself into the air and blasted toward the fading horizon.

Now you try:

Step Four: Editing and Sharing

Check your revision to see that all words are spelled correctly and that proper punctuation has been used. Then share your description.

Extension: Choose a piece of writing that you are working on. Try to add three or four adjectives.

Word Works V

1. **What do these words have in common?**

happily	sadly	gently	morosely
quietly	quickly	smoothly	mysteriously
slowly	angrily	raucously	peacefully

2. **What do these words have in common?**

never	very	too	somewhat
often	always	up	here
almost	also	not	later

Answer to Activities 1 and 2: The words are all ADVERBS.
Manner: *sadly, gently, smoothly*   **Place:** *here, up*   **Time:** *never, always, often*

■ What is an adverb?

■ Tell what you think an adverb is: _____

An ADVERB is a word that gives more information about a verb, an adverb, or an adjective. Many adverbs end with the letters -*ly*, but not all. Adverbs tell:

Where
The giant put the harp down *here* by the beanstalk. Snow White fell asleep *there* by the hut. The wolf lurks *nearby*.

Other words that can be adverbs that tell where are: outside, inside, away, up, down, near, far.

When
The wolf *often* spotted the pigs building their houses. The wolf *soon* devised a plan. The wolf approached the house of straw *later* in the afternoon.

Other words that can be adverbs that tell when are: now, then, soon, today, tomorrow, immediately, daily.

How
The wolf crept *quietly* toward the house. The wolf howled *happily* after he blew down the house of straw.

Other words that can be adverbs that tell how are: quite, stealthily, mysteriously, sadly, effortlessly, easily, sprightly.

How Often or How Long
The wolf *frequently* spied on the pigs. The wolf *sometimes* took a nap after eating. The wolf *never* tired of thinking of new tricks.

Other words that can be adverbs that tell how often or how long are: twice, thrice, always.

How Much

After lunch, the wolf was *too* full to move. The wolf was *somewhat* unsure that he could blow down the brick house. The wolf was *very* happy when he thought of a way to try and trick the third pig.

Other words that can be adverbs that tell how much are: hardly, rather, extremely, greatly, more, just, still.

Writing Activity I: *Adding Adverbs*

Add one or two adverbs to each of the following sentences.

EXAMPLES:

1. The frog croaked.
   The frog croaked *happily.* The frog croaked *grudgingly.*

2. The giant laughed.
   The giant laughed *loudly.* The giant laughed *heartily.*

3. The wolf howled.
   The wolf howled *yesterday.* The wolf *never* howled.

4. The ogre pushed.
   Yesterday, the ogre *easily* pushed his brother into the river.

Now you try:

5. **The hen clucked.**

   _____

   _____

6. **The princess sighed.**

   _____

   _____

7. **The seven dwarfs pulled.**

   _____

   _____

8. **The mermaid swam.**

   _____

   _____

Writing Activity II: *Speaking Adverbially*

Write a dialogue between two fairy-tale characters who are disagreeing about something. One character wants or thinks one thing; the other character wants or thinks something else. Be sure to use an adverb in each line. Here are some ideas to get you started:

- The frog wants to stay in the pond, but the princess wants him to go to the castle.

- The giant wants to climb down the beanstalk, but his wife wants him to stay home.

- Rumpelstiltskin doesn't want to spin any more straw into golden thread; the weaver's daughter wants him to one more time.

- The billy goat doesn't want to pay the troll's toll, but the troll demands it.

- The elf wants to dance on moonbeams; the sprite wants to watch fireflies.

EXAMPLE:

The mermaid wants to explore a shipwreck, but her friend wants to stay home and watch Jacques Cousteau on TV.

Mermaid: I <u>don't</u> want to stay <u>inside</u> tonight.

Friend: And I <u>don't</u> want to go <u>outside</u>.

Mermaid: Come on, we <u>always</u> do what you want.

Friend: I do <u>not</u> think so. We <u>never</u> do what I want.

Mermaid: <u>Yesterday</u>, we watched TV for rather a long time.

Friend: Yes, and we <u>almost</u> fell asleep.

Mermaid: I know; that show was <u>too</u> boring; I could not keep my eyes open. My eyes drooped <u>heavily</u>, like they were <u>suddenly</u> weighted with lead.

Friend: But you'll like tonight's show better. It's supposed to be <u>really</u> funny.

Mermaid: I still feel like I'm <u>endlessly</u> doing what you want.

Friend: Okay, just to show you that you're <u>not</u> <u>always</u> right, I'll <u>happily</u> go with you to explore that shipwreck.

Mermaid: You mean the one laying <u>mysteriously</u> in the canyon <u>nearly</u> five miles from here?

Friend: That very one.

- **Extension I:** Choose a piece of writing that you are working on. Try to add three or four adverbs.

- **Extension II:** Adding Details
  Begin with a verb. Add a noun. Add an adjective. Add another adjective. Add an adverb. For example:

Croak.	Laugh.
Frogs croak.	Elves laugh.
Happy frogs croak.	Forest elves laugh.
Happy leopard frogs croak.	Hidden forest elves laugh.
Happy leopard frogs croak musically.	Hidden forest elves laugh mysteriously.

Try your own.

Word Works VI

1. **What do these words have in common?**

about	below	for	throughout
above	beneath	from	to
across	beside	in	toward
on account of	in spite of	along with	together with

Answer to Activity 1: The words are all PREPOSITIONS.

■ What is a preposition?

■ Tell what you think a preposition is: _____

PREPOSITIONS are words that tell how nouns and pronouns relate to other words in a sentence or other parts of a sentence.

Here is a list of commonly used prepositions:

about	around	between	for	over	underneath
above	at	beyond	from	past	until
across	before	but ("except")	in	since	unto
after	behind	by	into	through	up
against	below	concerning	like	throughout	upon
along	beneath	down	of	to	with
amid	beside	during	off	toward	within
among	besides	except	on	under	without

■ A group of words may act as a preposition:

on account of   in spite of

along with   together with

■ A preposition usually introduces a phrase. The noun or pronoun (plus other words like adjectives) that follows the preposition is called "the object."

■ Some prepositions tell *when*: during, till, before, since, about, after, through, for.

■ Some prepositions tell *which*: with.

■ Some prepositions tell *what*: into.

■ Some prepositions tell *where*: above, across, around, behind, below, beside, next, in, underneath.

■ Some prepositions *compare things*: like, as.

Writing Activity I: *Placing Prepositions*

Prepositional phrases can appear at the beginning or at the end of a sentence. Add a prepositional phrase or two to the following sentences.

EXAMPLES:

1. The frog jumped. The frog on the lily pad (where) jumped into the rippling river (where).

2. The frog jumped. The frog with green spots (which) jumped away from the angry elf (where) during a thunderstorm (when).

3. The giant snored. In his bed (where), the giant snored throughout the night (when). The giant snored like a buzzsaw (comparison).

4. Rumpelstiltskin spun straw. Rumpelstiltskin spun straw in the room filled with straw (where). Rumpelstiltskin spun straw into golden thread (what).

Now you try:

5. **The queen laughed.**

_____

6. **The king called the guard.**

_____

7. **Snow White ate the poisoned apple.**

_____

8. **The bats flew.**

_____

Writing Activity II: *Replacing Words and Combining Sentences with Prepositions*

Rewrite and combine the following sentences by adding prepositional phrases. You may also add other words besides prepositions.

EXAMPLES:

1. There is a hen. There is a wooden table. The hen clucks and lays golden eggs.
   Perched *on the wooden table*, the hen clucks and lays golden eggs.

2. There is a giant. There is a beanstalk.
   The giant slid *down the beanstalk*.

3. There is a blackbird. There is a tree. There is a castle. There is a window.
   The blackbird flew *from the tree* and *through the castle window*.

4. There is an elf. There is a meadow. There is the moon.
   Alone *in the meadow*, the elf gazed *at the moon*.

Try your own:

5. There is a princess. There is a throne. There is a ballroom.

_____

6. There is a troll. There is a bridge.

_____

7. There is a dwarf. There is a shoe. The shoe looks like an ogre's foot.

_____

Writing Activity III: *Using Prepositions to Describe*

Look at a picture from a favorite children's picture book, or find a favorite painting, or choose a photograph from a newspaper or magazine. Use at least ten prepositions to describe what you see in the picture, painting, or photograph.

Example: A picture (the one where Max is running down the stairs) from *Where the Wild Things Are* by Maurice Sendak

Max is running *down the stairs*.
Max is running *toward the dog*.
Max has a fork *in his hand*.
Max's wolf suit has ears *on top of its head*.

Word Works VII

1. **What do these words have in common?**

and	but	or	yet
after	although	as	because
before	how	if	once
since	than	though	until

Answer to Activity 1: The words are all CONJUNCTIONS.

■ What is a conjunction?

■ Tell what you think a conjunction is: _____

A CONJUNCTION is a word that joins words or groups of words. Some conjunctions, called coordinating conjunctions, link words or independent clauses.

The giant *and* the troll gossiped about Rumpelstiltskin.
The giant likes to eat honey *and* vinegar sandwiches.
The dwarfs loved dancing on rooftops *and* singing to the stars.
The elf ran home, *for* he had forgotten the map to the treasure.
The queen promised to give Rumpelstiltskin a pardon, *yet* she smiled a cold *and* suspicious smile.
Jack took the cow to town, *and* he sold it for five beans.
Jack's mother took the beans, *but* she was unhappy.

Other conjunctions are called subordinating conjunctions; they introduce clauses. Here are some subordinating conjunctions that introduce adverbial clauses:

time	after, as, before, since, until, when, whenever, while
cause/reason	as, because, since, whereas
purpose/result	that, in order that, so that
condition	although, even though, unless, if, provided that, while

After the rain stopped, the giant jumped in the puddles.
Because the troll ran out of money, he had to charge a toll on his bridge.
So that she could continue to be the fairest in the land, the evil queen gave
    Snow White the apple.
Although she foiled Rumpelstiltskin's plans, the weaver's daughter avoided
    straw-filled rooms for the rest of her life.

Another kind of conjunction is called a correlative conjunction. Correlative conjunctions always are seen in pairs. Here are some common pairs of correlative conjunctions:

both . . . and
either . . . or
neither . . . nor
not only . . . but also
whether . . . or

Both the Wizard of Oz *and* Harry Potter are characters from well-known books.
Either the giant *or* the troll will be first in line at the mud pie eating contest.
Neither the dwarfs *nor* the local doctor could awaken Briar Rose from her deep sleep.
The elves brought *not only* moonbeam tea *but also* sweet ambrosia.
The giant exclaimed, "*Whether* you're ready *or* not, I'm coming to find you!"

Using conjunctions allows you to keep from writing a bunch of short, choppy sentences. When you use conjunctions, you make your sentences more interesting and you pull ideas together.

Writing Activity I: *Combining Sentences with Conjunctions*

Combine the following sentences with coordinating conjunctions.

EXAMPLES:

The evil queen went sailing. The troll went sailing.
The evil queen *and* the troll went sailing.

The elf bought rollerskates. The dwarf bought a skateboard.
The elf bought rollerskates, *and* the dwarf bought a skateboard.

Now you try:

1. The mermaid dove deeply. Her sister chased after small fish.

   _____

2. Baba Yaga lit the candles. Her cat slept in the corner.

   _____

3. The elf smiled. She said nothing.

   _____

4. Harry Potter phoned home. No one answered his call.

   _____

5. The king told the ogre, "You can stay. You can go home."

   _____

Writing Activity II: Creating Sentences with Conjunctions

Create sentences by using correlative conjunctions; use the words in each sentence.

EXAMPLES:

1. Hercules, Hydra
   In their battle, *either* Hercules *or* the Hydra would survive.

2. Icarus, his father
   Neither Icarus *nor* his father knew the wax that held the wings together would melt.

Now you try:

3. The third pig, the wolf

   _____

4. Cinderella, her stepmother

   _____

5. Giant, Jack

   _____

Writing Activity III: Revising Using Parts of Speech

Rewrite the following. Replace weak nouns and verbs with ones that are concrete and vivid. Add strong adjectives and adverbs. Add prepositional phrases. Add conjunctions (combine sentences) where needed. Here's an example:

> Orpheus got out of the boat. Orpheus was in front of a three-headed dog. The dog was not happy. Orpheus did not know what to do. Orpheus had an idea. He sang. The dog went to sleep.

> As he stepped out of the wood-splintered boat that had carried him across the cold, smooth river, Orpheus found himself facing a growling, three-headed dog. As the dog pawed the ground, each of its three heads opened their gaping mouths to reveal rows of yellow, jagged teeth. Each of the heads bit the air and howled a howl that shook the ground. Stunned and stymied, Orpheus froze like a statue of ice. With a thought that struck him like lightning, Orpheus stepped forward, tentatively, then he opened his mouth and began to sing softly. The growling menace grew silent. Its three heads turned sideways. As Orpheus continued his sweet melody, the terrible dog lay down, fell asleep, and snored softly.

Before you write your own story, tell how the revision is different from the original. Be specific. Talk about which words were changed; which words were added.

Rewrite this passage:

> The dragon was mad. The dragon landed on the ground. The dragon went to its cave. The dragon found that its treasure was missing. The dragon left the cave.

Sentence Works I

1. **What do these sentences have in common?**

   Eyes wide, mouth open, the troll stared at the third billy goat.

   Body quaking, hands trembling, Snow White dropped the apple.

   Radiator rattling, engine coughing, Cinderella's car came to a stop.

   Head back, hands raised, Jack stared in amazement at the huge beanstalk.

   Teeth bared, tongue flicking, the dragon eyed the approaching prince.

2. **What do these sentences have in common?**

   The sun having risen, the ogre dragged himself into his cave.

   The night being full of strange sounds, Red Riding Hood decided to stay home.

   The apple having been poisoned, Snow White fell asleep.

   The road having been blocked, Hercules rolled up his sleeves and started moving trees and boulders out of the way.

Answer to Activities 1 and 2: All the sentences begin with ABSOLUTE PHRASES.

■ What is an absolute phrase?

■ Tell what you think an absolute phrase is: _____

An ABSOLUTE PHRASE is a group of words (not a complete sentence) that usually gives more information about a noun or a pronoun. One kind of absolute phrase is made from a noun or pronoun plus a participle (a verb that ends with *-ing* or *-ed*), another kind is made from a noun and an adjective.

   Eyes wide, mouth open = noun + adjective
   Body quaking, hands trembling = noun + present participle
   Radiator rattling, engine coughing = noun + present participle
   Head back, hands raised = noun + adjective, noun + past participle

This kind of absolute phrase describes parts of a person, place, or thing.

Another kind of absolute contains linking verbs.

   The sun having risen = noun + linking verb + past participle
   The night being filled with strange sounds = noun + linking verb + past participle + prepositional phrase
   The apple having been poisoned = noun + linking verb + past participle
   The road having been blocked = noun + linking verb + past participle

This kind of absolute phrase shows cause; the rest of the sentence will describe the effect.

How to Create an Absolute Phrase That Describes

First, make a list of nouns that have moving parts in them: people, characters, animals, things that move or have moving parts.

The Brothers Grimm, Charles Perrault, J. K. Rowling
Hercules, Cinderella, Rapunzel
dragon, bat, goat, wolf, pig
cars, computer, house, carriage, bridge, castle

Second, choose one person, character, animal, or thing. Make a brief list of things that move on the person, character, animal, or thing.

Example: dragon

mouth opens	nostrils flare	head tilts down or up
wings flap	feet shift or shuffle	tail whips

Third, choose one or several parts of the person, animal, or thing that moves and add a present or past participle to it (separate absolute phrases with commas):

Head raised, mouth open, nostrils flaring, wings flapping, feet shuffling, the dragon roared.

How to Create an Absolute Phrase That Shows Cause and Effect

You can also make absolute phrases by placing a helping verb and a participle (both the helping verb and participle need to be either present or past) that show a cause for something in the second part of the sentence.

The fog being thick, Pegasus decided not to fly. (The thick fog is the cause of Pegasus's not flying.)

The fruit having turned brown and wrinkled, the dwarf decided to order a pizza. (The rotten fruit is the cause of the dwarf's decision to order pizza.)

The river being swift, the frog decided to stay on shore and bask in the sun.

The sun being bright, the ogre bought sunblock and sunglasses.

The forest having been burnt, Red Riding Hood wept.

Writing Activity: *Adding Absolutes*

Add absolute phrases to the following sentences. For sentences 1–4, add absolute phrases that describe (noun + participial); for sentences 5–7, add absolute phrases that show cause.

1. _____ , the queen cackled.

2. _____ , the giant bellowed.

3. _____ , the hen squawked.

4. _____ , the troll wept.

5. _____ , the carriage stopped.

6. _____ , the wolf growled.

7. _____ , Cinderella danced.

Create your own sentences with absolute phrases. Describe a favorite person, character, animal, or thing. You might try describing a picture or photograph.

Sentence Works II

1. **What do these sentences have in common?**

   Collecting tolls is the troll's favorite thing.

   Blowing down straw and stick houses is easy for the wolf.

   Looking into the magic mirror is something the evil queen does daily.

   Trying to get home was Odysseus' ten-year goal.

   Foretelling the future was the fortune-teller's trade.

2. **What do these sentences have in common?**

   The elf loved painting pictures with sunbeams.

   The dwarf spent long hours digging beneath the surface of the earth.

   Hercules labored long at completing his twelve tasks.

   The frog's favorite thing is submarining through still water.

   The princess's bane was talking to telemarketers on the royal phone.

Answer to Activities 1 and 2: All the sentences contain GERUND PHRASES.

■ What is a gerund phrase?

■ Tell what you think a gerund phrase is: _____

A GERUND PHRASE is a group of words (not a complete sentence) that acts like a noun. Gerund phrases begin with an *-ing* word; the *-ing* word is usually followed by a noun or a prepositional phrase. Gerund phrases can be the subject of a sentence, the subjective complement (if they follow a linking verb), the direct object (if they follow an action verb), or the object of a preposition.

Collecting tolls is the troll's favorite thing. (subject)
Blowing down straw and stick houses is easy for the wolf. (subject)
Hercules labored long at *completing his twelve tasks*. (object of the preposition "at")
The frog's favorite thing is *submarining through still water*. (subjective complement)
The elf loved *painting pictures with sunbeams*. (direct object)

How to Create Gerund Phrases

First, think of *-ing* words that can act like nouns: running, jumping, eating, fleeing, staring, holding, crossing, sleeping, and so on.

Second, think of the persons or animals that you associate with those *-ing* words: coyote, frog, Jack Sprat, etc.

Third, write a sentence that uses the *-ing* word (you can add more words after the *-ing* word) and is followed by a linking verb. These phrases will be the subjects of sentences.

Running a marathon was something the ogre would never do.
Jumping from pad to pad is the frog's version of an aerobic workout.
Staring into the eyes of a dragon can be frightening.

Gerund phrases can also be the objects of sentences that have action verbs as part of the predicate (the verb, though, usually shows something the subject of the sentence liked or disliked).

Harry Potter loved playing magical games.
Baba Yaga disliked having unwelcome visitors.
The wolf relished eating fresh bacon.

Gerund phrases can also be the objects of prepositions; usually the prepositions follow action verbs that are part of the predicate.

Hercules excelled at completing superhuman tasks.
Gnomes indulge in playing tricks on people.

Gerund phrases can also be subjective complements when they follow a linking verb.

Hercules' favorite thing is pumping iron.
The dwarfs exclaimed, "Look! Snow White is sleeping all the time."
The only thing the wolf loved was blowing down houses.

Writing Activity: A Gerund Poem

First, think of a book you have read, an event you have attended, or something else that has lots of people doing lots of things in the same place.

Example: fairy tales, a baseball stadium, a family gathering, an evening at the mall

Choose one place. Make a list of all the actions there. Describe those actions with gerund phrases.

Example: A baseball stadium: throwing fastballs, running bases, sliding home, calling strikes, hawking peanuts, watching fireworks, buying tickets, finding seats, yelling at the umpire, seeing your team win, going home happy

Second, begin with a statement like: A baseball stadium is. . . . When you want to introduce a new set of actions, repeat the line.

Third, list gerund phrases after the opening statement. Examples:

Baseball is . . .
buying tickets, pushing through throngs of spectators, searching for seats, waving pennants, munching peanuts
Baseball is . . .
throwing fastballs, belting triples, running bases, sliding home
Baseball is . . .
yelling at the umpire, leaping into the "wave," holding your breath as a home run barely clears the centerfield fence, watching fireworks burst overhead, pushing through the throng of baseball fans, going home happy

Try your own gerund poem.

Sentence Works III

1. **What do these sentences have in common?**

   To race rabbits was the turtle's burning wish.

   To escape from her tower of isolation was what Rapunzel wanted the most.

   To sing jazz tunes was something the ogre longed to do.

2. **What do these sentences have in common?**

   The troll hates to eat tofu.

   The genie loves to live life out of the bottle.

   Jason was driven to search for the golden fleece.

3. **What do these sentences have in common?**

   The princess wanted to upset the king, so she used his credit card.

   The frog leapt into the air to impress the princess.

   Pegasus was surprised to see a flock of winged goats.

   The giant bellowed to frighten Jack.

4. **What do these sentences have in common?**

   The wicked step sisters had a dress to suit every situation.

   The ogre created watercolor paintings to calm his foul mood.

   Orpheus struck upon an idea to solve his problem.

Answer to Activities 1 through 4: All the sentences contain INFINITIVE PHRASES.

- What is an infinitive phrase?

- Tell what you think an infinitive phrase is: _____

An INFINITIVE PHRASE is a group of words (not a complete sentence) that acts like a noun. Infinitive phrases begin with the word "to" followed by a verb. Infinitive phrases can be the subject of a sentence, a subjective complement (if they follow a linking verb), or a direct object (if they follow an action verb). Infinitive phrases can also act like adjectives and adverbs.

   To go home again was what Dorothy wanted most. (subject)

   Dorothy's utmost desire was to return to Kansas. (subjective complement)

   Dorothy hoped to see the flatlands of Kansas again. (direct object)

   Dorothy had an important question to ask the Wizard of Oz. (adjective; modifies question)

   Dorothy patiently listened to the Munchkins to mollify them. (adjective; modifies listened)

Writing Activity I: Using Infinitive Phrases

Turn these into complete sentences. A verb should follow each phrase.

1. **To spin straw into golden thread** _____.

   Example: To spin straw into golden thread was what the weaver's daughter wanted.

2. **To hoard gold** _____.

3. **To get to grandmother's house** _____.

4. **To be the fairest in the land** _____.

5. **To climb a beanstalk** _____.

Writing Activity II: An Infinitive Poem

First, think of characters from books you have read:

   Example: Rumpelstiltskin, Rapunzel, Dorothy, Harry Potter, Hansel

Second, choose one character.

   Example: the wolf (from "The Three Pigs")

Third, think of five things the character wanted and five things the character did not want. Use the infinitive form:

wanted	did not want
to blow down houses	to go hungry
to play tricks	to build a house
to eat three pigs	to eat just one pig
to get into the brick house	to be foiled by brick walls
to dream of bacon sandwiches	to become wolf stew

Fourth, choose three or four infinitive phrases from each list. Use them in a poem. The first stanza might begin with the line: All I wanted was. . . . Begin the second stanza with the line: But I didn't want. . . .

All I wanted was . . .
   to blow down houses
   to eat three pigs
   to dream of bacon sandwiches.

But I didn't want . . .
   to build a house
   to go hungry
   to be foiled by brick walls
   to become wolf stew.

Fifth, add adjectives to the phrases; change words; add additional phrases.

All I longed for was . . .
   to blow down flimsy, pork-hiding houses
   to lunch and munch on three plump pigs
   to doze the day away and digest a delectable meal
   to dream a delicious dream of succulent bacon sandwiches.

But I didn't want . . .
>   to labor, to sweat, to build a house of my own
>   to suffer the pangs of horrible hunger
>   to be foiled by a barrier of big brick walls
>   to slip down a chimney
>   to splash into a vat of water
>   to become wolf stew.

Try your own infinitive poem.

Sentence Works IV

1. **What do these sentences have in common?**
   The giant with one eye is the cyclops.
   The rotund egg on top of the wall tumbled to the ground.
   The girl in the next room fell asleep after eating a tainted apple.
   The frog near the princess used to be a prince.
   The book on the shelf is full of enchantments.

2. **What do these sentences have in common?**
   Pegasus flew over the crumbling castle.
   Jack climbed up the beanstalk.
   The giant yelled at Jack.
   The gremlin scurried through the forest.
   The elf swung from tree to tree.

Answer to Activities 1 and 2: All the sentences contain PREPOSITIONAL PHRASES.

■ What is a prepositional phrase?

■ Tell what you think a prepositional phrase is: _____

A PREPOSITIONAL PHRASE is a group of words (not a complete sentence) that is made of a preposition plus an object. Prepositional phrases usually act like nouns, adjectives, or adverbs.

Prepositional phrases that act like adjectives:
>   The wolf *in the next room* wants to become a vegetarian. (modifies wolf)
>   The snorting dragon *in the cave* has a toothache. (modifies dragon)
>   The troll *beneath the bridge* is a green, greedy fellow. (modifies troll)
>   The city *beyond the horizon* is called Oz. (modifies city)

Prepositional phrases that act like adverbs:

The ranting ogre flung the mug *across the room.* (modifies flung)

The dimpled dragon blew smoke *through his teeth.* (modifies blew)

Hercules grabbed the horrible hydra *by the nose.* (modifies grabbed)

The dwarfs looked *to the sky.* (modifies looked)

The frog flipped *into the pond.* (modifies flipped)

Prepositional phrases that act like nouns (when a prepositional phrase is the subject of a sentence, it is followed by a linking verb):

Beneath the bridge is the place where the troll lives. (subject)

In the giant's fisted hand was the key to the treasure chamber. (subject)

In the dark, dark cave is where Hansel's cousin got lost. (subject)

"*Out of here is where I long to be!*" exclaimed the weaver's daughter. (subject)

Writing Activity: *The Preposition Poem*

First, think of an animal, character, or object that is very active: a bird, a frog, an elf, a bouncing ball, etc.

Second, choose one: for example, a nightingale.

Third, choose five to ten prepositions (refer to the list of prepositions given in Chapter 1, Word Works VI); for example, in, on, below, above, beneath, through, beside, beyond, etc.

Fourth, write a poem in which you tell all the places your subject goes; use prepositional phrases. Begin with the line: The nightingale flew. (tell where it went)

> The nightingale flew
>> to the forest, through the trees,
>> across the swamp, near an ogre,
>> around the horn of a unicorn, toward a giant,
>> between a pair of bats, beneath a bridge,
>> away from a pair of elves, beyond the reach of a gremlin.

Fifth, add strong adjectives:

> The nightingale flew
>> into the enchanted forest, through the thick tangle of trees,
>> across the smoldering swamp, near a sleeping ogre,
>> around the shiny horn of a unicorn, toward a grumpy giant,
>> between a pair of gossiping bats, beneath the troll's battered bridge,
>> away from a pair of acrobatic elves,
>> beyond the reach of a gruesome gremlin, into the dusky twilight.

Try your own preposition poem.

Sentence Works V

1. **What do these sentences have in common?**

   The giant winking his one eye is a cyclops.

   The rotund egg teetering on the wall tumbled to the ground.

   The girl eating a tainted apple will soon fall asleep.

   The frog croaking near the princess used to be a prince.

   Puffing smoke and flaring his nostrils, the dragon groaned with indigestion.

2. **What do these sentences have in common?**

   Startled by a flock of goats with wings, Pegasus headed for home.

   Fueled with a sense of injustice, Jack climbed up the beanstalk.

   Inflamed with anger, the giant yelled at Jack.

   The gremlin, frightened by a bunch of bats,
   scurried through the forest.

   The elf, intoxicated with joy, swung from tree to tree.

Answer to Activities 1 and 2: All the sentences contain PARTICIPIAL PHRASES.

- What is a participial phrase?

- Tell what you think a participial phrase is: _____

A PARTICIPIAL PHRASE is a group of words (not a complete sentence) that is made of a present participle (an *-ing* word) or a past participle (an *-ed* word). Participial phrases act like adjectives because they give more information about a noun or pronoun. In participial phrases, the participle is often followed by a noun, an adverb, or a prepositional phrase. Participles at the beginning of the sentence end with a comma.

Present participles:

The wolf *reading a nonmeat cookbook* wants to become a vegetarian. (modifies wolf)

Groaning and moaning, the dragon complained about a toothache. (modifies dragon)

The troll *fuming beneath the bridge* is a green, greedy fellow. (modifies troll)

Grinding his teeth, flailing his arms, and stamping his feet, the dwarf refused to eat his broccoli. (modifies dwarf)

Past participles:

The ranting ogre, *disgusted with the taste of his drink,* flung the mug of mud across the room. (modifies ogre)

Amused at what he read in his comic book, the dimpled dragon blew streams of smoke through his teeth. (modifies dragon)

Banished from Mount Olympus, Hercules found a job as a rodeo clown. (modifies Hercules)

Filled with wonder, the dwarfs looked to the sky. (modifies dwarfs)

The frog, *fixated by his reflection,* flipped into the pond. (modifies frog)

Writing Activity I: *Adding Participles*

Add two or three present participial phrases to the following sentences. Be sure to tell, with -*ing* phrases, what the subject of each sentence is doing.

EXAMPLES:

1. _____ ,

    the giant fell asleep.

    Yawning widely, stretching his arms grotesquely, and sighing deeply, the giant fell asleep.

2. _____ ,

    the weaver's daughter wept.

    Eyeing the enormous size of her task and plopping herself down on the straw-strewn floor, the weaver's daughter wept.

3. _____ ,

    the wizened old man vanished.

    Whispering odd words under his breath and tapping his cane to the ground, the wizened old man vanished.

Now you try:

4. _____ ,

    the queen stepped into the room.

5. _____ ,

    the princess looked at her broken crown.

6. _____ ,

    Rapunzel ran to the window.

7. _____ ,

    the dwarf was a great cook.

8. The ogre, _____ ,

    stomped into the room.

9. The mean queen, _____ ,

    grabbed the magic mirror.

10. The elf, _____ ,

    couldn't believe his eyes.

Writing Activity II: *Beginning with Participles*

Write three sentences. Include two different participial phrases from the following list in each sentence. The phrases should go before the subject (noun).

Humming like a hive of bees	Hidden in the attic
Gazing into the magic mirror	Moping morosely
Wringing her hands	Overcome with laughter
Glued to the spot	Looking like a faded flower
Lost forever	Jumping up and down
Dancing like lightning	Filled with fear
Dangling from a castle ledge	Ducking under the drawbridge
Croaking and crooning	Covered with soot and ash
Gripping the sceptre	Shuddering with anxiety
Frowning and glowering	Stuffing magic marbles into boxes
Perched on an oak branch	Rusted by rain

Special Focus: Dangling Participles

Dangling Participle: A participial phrase that begins a sentence and does not connect to the noun or pronoun that is the subject of the sentence is a dangling participle. When participial phrases at the beginning of the sentence don't give information about the subject of the sentence, the sentence will not make sense.

The first sentence contains a dangling participle; the second sentence has been rewritten and uses the participial phrase correctly.

Bellowing, fuming, and snorting smoke, the forest was burned. (Was the forest bellowing, fuming, and snorting?)

Bellowing, fuming, and snorting smoke, the dragon watched the forest burn.

Checking the weather, the gray clouds moved to the east. (Are the clouds checking the weather?)

Checking the weather, the Oz meteorologist said that the gray clouds were moving to the east.

Getting ready to land, the dwarf on the ground motioned to Pegasus. (Is the dwarf getting ready to land?)

Getting ready to land, Pegasus looked to the dwarf motioning on the ground.

Looking up from below, the egg on the tower tumbled to the ground. (Is the egg looking up?)

Looking up from below, all the king's horses and all the king's men watched in horror as the egg tumbled to the ground.

Rewriting Sentences to Reconnect Dangling Participles

Rewrite the following sentences so that the participial phrases in them make sense. You may need to add words, especially nouns as subjects.

1. Shattered beyond repair, the ogre spotted his favorite mug on the floor.

   _____

2. Bolted with a padlock, the prince could not open the castle door.

   _____

3. Smiling a smile as large as the moon, the music played while the princess danced.

   _____

4. Shaking and sweating with fear, the wolf approached as the first pig watched with wide eyes.

   _____

5. Holding his breath, the room filled with smoke as the prince tried to escape.

   _____

Sentence Works VI

1. **What do these sentences have in common?**

   Snow White, the innocent girl, loved apples.

   Cinderella, the unlucky lass, was mistreated by her stepmother and stepsisters.

   Pegasus, the white winged horse, flew from Athens to Sparta.

   Rumpelstiltskin, that mysterious and magical being, spun straw into golden thread.

   Rapunzel, the long-haired lass, longed to be released from her tower.

   The wolf, that ever-hungry creature prowling the edge of the forest, preyed upon lazy pigs.

> **Answer to Activity 1: All the sentences contain APPOSITIVE PHRASES.**

■ What is an appositive phrase?

■ Tell what you think an appositive phrase is: _____

> An APPOSITIVE PHRASE is a group of words (not a complete sentence) that follows a noun that is often the subject of the sentence. An appositive phrase restates the noun; it gives more precise information about the noun it follows. Many appositive phrases are made of an article (a, an, the) plus an adjective plus a noun. Appositive phrases can also include participial phrases, prepositional phrases, infinitive phrases, and clauses. Commas separate the appositive phrase from the rest of the sentence.
>
> Jack, *the bold thief,* absconded with the giant's bag of gold. (adjective + noun)
> Jack, *the stealthy thief creeping through the doorway,* absconded with the giant's bag of gold (adjective + noun + participial phrase)

Jack, *the brazen thief near the beanstalk,* absconded with the giant's bag of gold. (adjective + noun + prepositional phrase)

Jack, *the thief to admire,* absconded with the giant's bag of gold. (noun + infinitive)

Jack, *the wily thief who outsmarted his large foe,* absconded with the giant's bag of gold. (adjective + noun + adjective clause)

Jack, *the thief who crept into the huge house while holding his breath,* absconded with the giant's bag of gold. (noun + adjective clause + gerund phrase)

Writing Activity I: *Adding Appositives*

Add an appositive phrase to each of the following sentences:

EXAMPLES:

1. **Achilles fought during the Trojan War.**

   Achilles, *a powerful Greek warrior,* fought during the Trojan War.

   Achilles, *the Greek warrior with only one weak spot on his body,* fought during the Trojan War.

   Achilles, *the stalwart warrior who often sulked when he didn't get what he wanted,* fought during the Trojan War.

2. **Hector was Achilles' enemy.**

   Hector, *the breaker of horses,* was Achilles' enemy.

Now you try:

3. **Rapunzel languished in her tower.**

   _____

   _____

4. **Cinderella loved glass shoes.**

   _____

   _____

5. **Snow White loved applesauce.**

   _____

   _____

6. **Gretel dropped bread crumbs in the forest.**

   _____

   _____

Sentence Works VII

1. **What do these sentences have in common?**

   The spell that enchanted Briar Rose lasted for one hundred years.

   The girl who claimed to be Briar Rose's long-lost sister was an impostor.

   The troll, who plays tag with gargoyles, fell in love with her own reflection.

   The spinning wheel, which Rumpelstiltskin used to spin straw into golden thread, was stolen from the Fairy Tale Museum last night.

   Baba Yaga dashed to the swamp where the fireflies are as large as bats.

   The tooth that hangs from the chain around the queen's neck once belonged to a dragon.

   Answer to Activity 1: All the sentences contain ADJECTIVE CLAUSES.

   ■ What is an adjective clause?

   ■ Tell what you think an adjective clause is: _____

   An ADJECTIVE CLAUSE is a group of words that has a subject and a predicate. An adjective clause is not a complete sentence, however, because it cannot stand alone. Adjective clauses give more information about a noun or pronoun.

   Adjective clauses usually begin with *who, whom, whose, which, that, when* (if the sentence has a linking verb as the predicate), or *where*; these words are followed by a *verb* (the verb may be followed by other words such as nouns and prepositional phrases).

   The princess *who wears size twelve shoes* won the royal foot race. (modifies princess)
   The princess, *who has never been to El Paso*, is studying the map. (modifies princess)
   Snow White was the innocent heroine *whom the dwarfs had guarded for a decade.* (modifies heroine)
   Vasilisa was the girl *to whom the secret treasure was given.* (modifies girl)
   The evil queen was startled to see the prince, *whose head was too big for a hat*, wearing a crown as big as a wagon wheel. (modifies prince)
   Every night the troll read "The Little Mermaid," *which was penned by Hans Christian Andersen.* (modifies "The Little Mermaid")
   The frog finally found the golden orb, *which has been stuck in the bottom of the well for nineteen years.* (modifies orb)
   The strange words *that were scribbled on the scroll* were written by an obscure elf. (modifies words)
   Tonight is the night *when gargoyles come to life.* (modifies night)
   The ogre found the field *where pickles grow to the size of watermelons.* (modifies field)

Writing Activity I: *Adding Adjective Clauses*

Add an adjective clause to each of the following:

EXAMPLES:

1. **The troll trudged through the swamp.**
   The troll, *who won last night's spelling bee*, trudged through the swamp.
2. **The princess reached for the shimmering jewel.**
   The princess reached for the shimmering jewel *which fell from her crown*.

Now you try:

3. **The wolf discovered the place. (where . . .)**

   _____

4. **The elf sat alone. (The elf who . . . sat alone.)**

   _____

5. **The hobbit carried a magical sword. (which . . .)**

   _____

6. **The hobbit climbed the mountain. (who . . .)**

   _____

7. **Harry Potter found the key. (that . . .)**

   _____

Writing Activity II: *Adding Adjective Clauses*

Revise the following by adding adjective clauses.

Dear Cinderella,

You won't believe what has happened recently. I met the Wizard of Oz, who

_____.

He told me about a pair of magic shoes, which

_____.

But he said that the only place I could find them was in a castle where

_____.

I plan to go to that castle tonight when

_____.

Wish me luck.

Your friend, Dorothy.

Sentence Works VIII

1. **What do these sentences have in common?**

   Before it flew from its cave, the dragon waxed its wings.

   Baba Yaga lived where no one else did.

   Because the ogre was cranky, he refused to answer the telephone.

   Since twenty bats were circling overhead, the king decided not to wear his Dracula costume.

   The evil queen enchanted another apple, even though she knew the attempt was hopeless.

   Harry Potter and his friends spoke in hushed tones so that they would not disturb the sleeping, three-headed dog.

   The hobbit climbed the mountain so that he could dispose of the ring.

   Unless the hobbit threw the ring into the volcanic fire, the world would be overrun by dark forces.

Answer to Activity 1: All the sentences contain ADVERBIAL CLAUSES.

- What is an adverbial clause?
- Tell what you think an adverbial clause is: _____

An ADVERBIAL CLAUSE is a group of words that has a subject and a predicate. An adverbial clause is not a complete sentence, however, because it cannot stand alone. Adverbial clauses give more information about a verb, an adjective, or an adverb. Adverbial clauses tell time, cause or reason, purpose or result, or condition; they begin with subordinating conjunctions:

time:	after, before, since, until, when, whenever, while
place:	where, wherever
cause/reason:	as, because, since, whereas
purpose:	in order that, so that
result:	that, so
condition:	although, even though, unless, if, provided that, while

Time

Whenever the sky turns grey and green, the ogres gather to cavort.

Before the sun sets, the gremlins will all put on their masks.

The frog will not give back the golden orb *until the princess apologizes.*

After Ajax won the race, Achilles sat in his tent and sulked.

While the Trojans were sleeping, Odysseus silently slipped out of the big, wooden horse.

Place

The gnome slept *wherever he could.*

Wherever he went, the hobbit found signs of impending doom.

Cause/Reason

Because no one could pull the sword from the stone, Arthur decided to try.

As no one seemed to be home, the wolf crept inside the cottage.

Since he was still hungry, the wolf loped to the second pig's house.

Purpose

The ogre ate the map *so that no one else could find the magic fountain.*

The dragon bellowed *in order that he might frighten the tourists.*

Result

The wolf was so ornery *that he changed into grandmother's clothes.*

Achilles was angry, *so he decided to sulk.*

Condition

Although the gremlins have never won a game, they keep hoping.

Even though the ogres had a bake sale, no one bought their brick cakes.

Unless it snows, the elves cannot wear their snowshoes.

Writing Activity I: *Adding Adverbial Clauses*

Add an adverbial clause to each of the following:

EXAMPLES:

1. The troll trudged through the swamp.

   The troll trudged through the swamp *because the bridge had collapsed.*

2. The princess reached for the shimmering jewel.

   Since she was enthralled, the princess reached for the shimmering jewel.

Now you try:

3. The wolf's stomach rumbled.

   _____

4. The elf sat alone.

   _____

5. The hobbit carried a magical sword.

   _____

6. The hobbit climbed the mountain.

   _____

7. Harry Potter lost the secret key.

   _____

Writing Activity II: Building with Adverbial Clauses

Add a sentence to the following adverbial clauses:

EXAMPLES:

1. **Although the door was locked . . .**
   Although the door was locked, the gremlin kept trying to turn the knob.

2. **Before the princess had time to blink . . .**
   Before the princess had time to blink, the stooped, old woman disappeared in a puff of smoke.

Now you try:

3. **Since the drawbridge was down . . .**
   _____

4. **. . . even though the room was dark.**
   _____

5. **. . . although he was smiling. (be sure the subject refers to "he")**
   _____

6. **When the moon is full . . .**
   _____

7. **In order that he might impress the king . . .**
   _____

Sentence Works IX

1. **What do these sentences have in common?**
   That Briar Rose was snoring loudly was what the prince noticed.
   The prince suspected that Briar Rose was allergic to roses.
   The prince's greatest fear was that Briar Rose wouldn't like his cologne.
   The prince thought that he was in the wrong castle.
   The prince's preparation for what he thought he might find served him well.
   The prince wondered why Briar Rose had fallen asleep.

Answer to Activity 1: All the sentences contain NOUN CLAUSES.

■ What is a noun clause?

■ Tell what you think a noun clause is: _____

A NOUN CLAUSE is a group of words that has a subject and a predicate. A noun clause is not a complete sentence, however, because it cannot stand alone. A noun clause acts like a noun and can be the subject, the subjective complement (a clause that follows a linking verb), or the direct object of a sentence; it can also be the object of a preposition.

Subject

That the elf was amused was clear.

What the dwarf reported was startling.

Why the ogre wore tap-dancing shoes remains a mystery.

Whoever forecasted rain was wrong.

Subjective Complement

The king's concern was *that his daughter would become a rock star.*

Achilles's greatest hope was *that he would win the next race.*

Ajax's chief suspicion is *that Achilles will cheat.*

Direct Object

Achilles knows *that Ajax thinks he will cheat.*

The elf did not believe *what the dwarf reported.*

The evil queen knows *why the ogre wore tap-dancing shoes.*

Snow White asked *whomever she could* about the history of apples.

The queen asked *where the princess was.*

Object of a Preposition

The hobbit was nervous about *what Golum said.*

Baba Yaga's understanding of *what the ogre said* helped her set a trap.

Baba Yaga listened to *what the ogre reported.*

Writing Activity I: *Building with Noun Clauses*

Add a sentence to the following noun clauses:

EXAMPLES:

1. **That the magician was a fraud ...**

   That the magician was a fraud was evident to the howling harpies.

2. **... that the harpies couldn't be trusted.**

   The evil queen thought *that the harpies couldn't be trusted.*

Now you try:

3. **Whichever ogre chose canned spinach for lunch ...**

_____

4. What Achilles said . . .

_____

5. . . . that Odysseus was lost.

_____

6. . . . why Circe changed Odysseus' men into pigs.

_____

7. . . . what the dwarf sang.

_____

Writing Activity II: Writing with Noun Clauses

Add noun clauses:

Rapunzel knows that _____.

But Rumpelstiltskin wondered what _____.

And theWizard of Oz knows why _____.

_____ was evident to the Wicked Witch of the West.

_____ was startling to the Munchkins.

_____ remains a secret.

Sentence Expanding

There are four basic sentence patterns:

1. **noun + verb (intransitive—the verb does not carry the action over to an indirect or direct object)**
   - Rapunzel laughed.
   - Cinderella weeps.
   - Nightingales warble.
   - The dragon slept.

2. **noun + verb (transitive—the verb carries over to a direct or indirect object) + noun**
   - Ajax won the race.
   - The magician hurled the orb.
   - Ogres eat weeds.
   - The orb frightened the rabbit.

3. **noun + linking verb + noun**
   - Dragons are reptiles.
   - Rapunzel is a veterinarian.
   - Frogs are amphibians.
   - Fog is mist.

4. **noun + linking verb + adjective**
   - Dragons are green.
   - The gremlin was persistent.
   - The wolf was fierce.
   - The bat is acrobatic.

Sentences can be expanded by adding information to the subject, the verb, the object of the verb, the predicate noun, or the subjective complement (the beginning, the middle, or the end of the sentence).

Examples of sentence expansion at the beginning:

Rapunzel smiled.

Silly Rapunzel smiled. (adjective)

Rapunzel, the lonely girl in the tower, smiled. (appositive phrase + prepositional phrase)

Holding the letter in her hand, Rapunzel smiled. (participial phrase)

To her own great surprise, Rapunzel smiled. (prepositional phrase)

Rapunzel, who loves frogs, smiled. (adjective clause)

Her eyes dancing, Rapunzel smiled. (absolute phrase)

Examples of sentence expansion at the end:

Rapunzel smiled.

Rapunzel smiled a smile that was as large as half a pizza. (adjective clause)

Rapunzel smiled righteously. (adverb)

Rapunzel smiled to herself. (prepositional phrase)

Rapunzel smiled to show her approval (infinitive phrase)

Rapunzel smiled like a frog nabbing a fly. (prepositional phrase + gerund phrase)

Rapunzel smiled, nervously at first, then with growing abandon. (adverbs + prepositional phrases)

Rapunzel smiled while holding her breath. (preposition + participial phrase)

Rapunzel smiled, then she began blowing up balloons. (adverbial clause + gerund phrase)

Rapunzel smiled more often than her benign captor wanted her to. (adverb + adverbial clause)

Rapunzel smiled since she had nothing better to do. (adverbial clause + infinitive phrase)

Rapunzel smiled because she could not contain her joy. (adverbial clause)

Writing Activity: Expanding Sentences

Effective writers often do not tell the reader what a character is feeling; they show by using concrete details. Rewrite the following to "show" how the character is feeling. Eliminate any abstract nouns or adjectives. Use vivid nouns and verbs; use phrases and clauses.

EXAMPLES:

1. The ogre was angry. (Get rid of the word "angry" and paint a word picture that shows the ogre's anger.)

   Eyes bulging, face twisted, the ogre stamped the ground and pounded on the bolted, rough-hewn door with his white-hot fists.

2. The owl flew.

   Gliding through the tangled forest on silent wings, the owl hooted a ghostly hoot and disappeared into the darkness.

Now you try:

3. Bullfrogs croak. (Why do they croak? Where do they croak? How do they croak? What causes them to croak? When do they croak?)

   _____

4. The queen screamed. (Why did she scream? Where did she scream? How did she scream? What caused her to scream? When did she scream?)

   _____

5. Cinderella was sad.

   _____

6. Rapunzel was ecstatic.

   _____

7. The princess was bored.

   _____

8. The dragon went away.

   _____

9. The minotaur bellowed.

   _____

10. Sleeping Beauty was confused.

   _____

11. The gargoyle came into the room.

   _____

12. The wolf growled.

   _____

Sentence Combining

Some short sentences are good. They can be strong. They can be jazzy. They can be easy to read. They can be easy to understand. But they can be really boring (just like these sentences).

What puts the music and meaning into writing? Sentence variety. Well-wrought sentences. Sentences that have flair.

Good writers combine the six phrases and three clauses to create sentences that zing and pop. Their sentences are like poetry; they slide across the page and slip like sweet music into the mind.

See the difference between the following sets of writing. The short-sentence combinations are choppy, like jackhammers. The revisions of those short sentences are smoother and tastier.

Combine the following sentences by using participial phrases:

EXAMPLES:

1. **Rapunzel frets. Rapunzel sweats. Rapunzel grabs the rail. Rapunzel longed for a better life.**
   Fretting, sweating, and grabbing the rail, Rapunzel longed for a better life.

2. **The ogre strains against the boulder. The ogre pushes with all his might. The ogre digs in his horn-toed feet. The ogre growled with determination.**
   Straining against the boulder, pushing with all his might, digging in his horn-toed feet, the ogre growled with determination.

Now you try:

3. **The queen threw up her hands. The queen signaled the band. The queen stepped onto the dance floor. The queen was the belle of the ball.**

   _____

   _____

4. **The elves crowded together. The elves smiled in amazement. The elves sang secret songs. The elves welcomed the stranger.**

   _____

   _____

Combine by using absolute phrases:

EXAMPLES:

5. **His eyes were narrow. His fists were clenched. The gremlin snarled.**
   Eyes narrow, fists clenched, the gremlin snarled.

6. **His feet were planted. His mind was set. The prince raised his shield against the oncoming dragon.**

   _____

   _____

How many ways can you combine the following sentences?

EXAMPLES:

1. The dwarfs were weary. They set down their burden. They sighed with relief. They marveled that they had reached the end of their journey.

   Marveling that they had reached the end of their journey, the weary dwarfs set down their burden and sighed with relief.

   Setting down their burden, sighing with relief, the weary dwarfs marveled that they had reached the end of their journey.

2. The magician's eyes sparkled. The magician gloated. He had hoodwinked the king. He readied himself for the next deception.

   Having hoodwinked the king, the magician gloated with sparkling eyes as he readied himself for the next deception.

   Eyes sparkling, the magician gloated, after having hoodwinked the king, and prepared himself for the next deception.

Now you try:

3. Cinderella was asleep in her dingy bed. Cinderella was dreaming. She was dreaming of royal balls and glass slippers. She was dreaming of a life without ashes.

   _____

   _____

   _____

4. The royal carriage jerked along the rocky road. The carriage lurched. The carriage bounced. The wheels of the carriage squeaked.

   _____

   _____

   _____

5. The swamp was endless. The hobbits trudged. The hobbits sloshed. The hobbits were frightened. The hobbits were lost.

   _____

   _____

   _____

6. The room was filled with straw. There were rats in the corner. There were spiderwebs covering the windows. The walls were a dingy gray. Bats hung from the ceiling.

   _____

   _____

   _____

Sentence Matching

Sentence Matching I

Match the beginning of each sentence in column 1 with its appropriate ending in column 2. Note that there are seven sentence beginnings and eight sentence endings (one ending does not belong).

a. By the time her stepmother came home,

b. The wolf didn't go out for dinner because

c. The frogs always gather

d. The ogre had been hypnotically staring into the flame

e. The gremlin refused to speak to the evil queen

f. Achilles has never

g. The troll needed money

_____ been to El Paso.

_____ for over a week.

_____ while the bats hung from the trees.

_____ because to liked to gamble on the rat races.

_____ at the pond on the first full moon of each month.

_____ Cinderella had scrubbed the entire house.

_____ until she agreed to apologize.

_____ he had filled up on pork earlier in the day.

■ How did you make your decisions?

■ What knowledge about phrases and clauses helped you?

Sentence Matching II

Match the beginning of each sentence in column 1 with its appropriate ending in column 2. Note that there are seven sentence beginnings and eight sentence endings (one ending does not belong).

a. Upon hearing his name spoken aloud,

b. After seeing how enormous her task was,

c. The weaver's daughter, who had become the queen, was so desperate

d. After the queen failed to name him,

e. Although she stayed up all night long thinking and thinking,

f. While Rumpelstiltskin spun straw into golden thread,

g. Rumpelstiltskin spun straw for the weaver's daughter

_____ she could not come up with the little man's name.

_____ the weaver's daughter slept.

_____ because he wanted something from her.

_____ the little man laughed.

_____ the little man shrieked.

_____ until she agreed to apologize.

_____ the weaver's daughter plopped down and wept.

_____ that she sent her loyal handmaiden into the forest to search for the little man's name.

■ How did you make your decisions?

■ What knowledge about phrases and clauses helped you?

Sentence Sense

1. Write a sentence that begins with two participial phrases.

    _____

    _____

2. Write a sentence that begins with two absolute phrases.

    _____

    _____

3. Write a sentence that has an appositive phrase.

    _____

    _____

4. Write a sentence that has an infinitive phrase.

    _____

    _____

5. Write a sentence that begins with a gerund phrase.

    _____

    _____

6. Write a sentence that has two prepositional phrases.

    _____

    _____

7. Write a sentence that begins with an adverbial clause.

    _____

    _____

8. Write a sentence that has an adjective clause.

    _____

    _____

9. Write a sentence that has a participial phrase and an adjective clause.

    _____

    _____

10. Write a sentence that has two prepositional phrases and an adverbial clause.

    _____

    _____

11. Write a sentence that has an appositive phrase and ends with an adverbial clause.

    _____

    _____

12. Write a sentence that has an absolute phrase, an infinitive phrase, and an adverbial clause.

    _____

    _____

Punctuation Points

The Comma

Common Uses:

1. **To separate two or more adjectives before a noun:**
   The shiny, red, ripe apple dripped with poison.

2. **To separate words or groups of words in a series:**
   They saw Cinderella scrubbing the stove, washing the windows, digging soot out of the fireplace, and painting the hen's feet with nail polish.
   The bat swooped through the living room, into the fireplace, and out the chimney.
   The party was filled with guests like ogres, gremlins, centaurs, elves, and giants.

3. **To separate opening phrases in sentences:**
   After a ride through the countryside, the prince returned to the castle to play checkers.
   Knees knocking, the princess trembled as she opened the glowing door.
   Sagging with exhaustion, Hercules sat down after completing his twelfth task.

4. **To separate a phrase that interrupts the main thought in a sentence:**
   Snow White was, in the evil queen's opinion, too pretty and too spunky.
   Snow White, the spunky lass who lived alone in the forest, had never looked into a mirror.

5. **To separate two complete sentences with a connecting word (conjunction):**
   The ogre could try to sell beauty products, or he could try to work for the phone company.
   The prince tried to slay the dragon, but he was unsuccessful.
   The hobbit grabbed the ring, and he realized he had made a mistake.

6. **To introduce a quotation in a sentence:**
   Every day the queen gazed into the mirror and asked, "Mirror, mirror on the wall, who's the fairest of them all?"
   The giant bellowed, "Fee, fie, fo, fum, I smell the blood of an Englishman!"

7. **To separate the day from the year in a date:**
   July 7, 1777

8. **To separate a city from a state:**
   El Paso, Texas
   St. Louis, Missouri

9. **To separate a person's name and title:**
   Cinderella, Director of House Cleaning
   Chief of Ogres United, Blaine Uther
   Oz CEO, J. Scarecrow

10. **To introduce a personal letter:**
    Dear Rapunzel,

The Apostrophe

Common Uses:

1. **To show contractions:**
   would not = wouldn't
   is not = isn't
   it is = it's
   will not = won't

2. **To show that something belongs to someone:**
   Cinderella's foul luck
   The queen's mirror

   To show that something belongs to more than one person:
   the elves' magic
   the gremlins' rowboat
   the deer's hiding places

The Colon

Common Uses:

1. **To show a list is coming:**
   Cinderella disliked many things: sweeping soot, scrubbing floors, painting hen's feet, repairing the roof, herding the horses, and staying at home alone.

2. **To introduce a business letter:**
   Dear Director of Oz, Inc.:
   Dear Sir:

The Exclamation Point

Common Use:

To show surprise, excitement, anger, or fear:
Oh no!
Yikes!
The ogre said, "Now I've got you!"

Quotation Marks

Common Use:

To show who is speaking:

"Cinderella! Where are you?" shrieked the stepmother.

"I don't believe we've met," said the queen to Snow White, "but I'm very happy to meet you."

The Semicolon

Common Use:

To join two independent clauses:

Cinderella desperately desired to go to the ball; her sisters wanted her to stay home.

The giant lumbered after Jack; Jack scampered down the beanstalk.

Special Focus: The Comma Splice

When a comma is used in place of a semicolon, it is called a "comma splice." A comma splice is an incorrect way to use a comma; it is a usage error. Remember, a semicolon must connect two independent clauses; a comma cannot.

Here are examples of comma splices:

Splice: Cinderella searched for love, Jack searched for gold.
No Splice: Cinderella searched for love; Jack searched for gold.

Splice: The elves were wide-eyed, they stood in amazement as the balloon landed.
No Splice: The elves were wide-eyed; they stood in amazement as the balloon landed.

Splice: Cinderella jumped into the coach, she had no other way to get to the palace.
No Splice: Cinderella jumped into the coach; she had no other way to get to the palace.

The Hyphen

Common Uses:

1. **To separate numbers from twenty-one to ninety-nine**

2. **To use with prefixes ex-, self-, all-, and with prefixes before all proper nouns and adjectives; and with the suffix -elect:**
   ex-president   president-elect   self-deception   sub-Saharan

3. **To separate compound words when they operate as adjectives before a noun:**
   a well-designed plan   a well-rendered portrait

The Dash

Common Uses:

1. **To show a sudden shift in thought:**
   The giant reached for Jack—and here's where the story gets weird—and offered him a fish.

2. **To separate words that normally might appear in a parenthesis:**
   Few folktales—roughly seven in number—have unhappy endings.

3. **To indicate an element that explains or emphasizes something in the sentence, such as *namely, in other words, that is,* etc.**
   Achilles fought in the Trojan War for only one reason—fame.

What Is a Sentence?

A sentence is a group of words that express a complete thought. For this group of words to express a complete thought, it must have both a subject and a predicate. The subject is the word or words that are the main topic of the sentence; the predicate is the word or words that tell what the subject is doing or what condition the subject is in.

Each of the following words and groups of words is NOT a sentence:

Cinderella
Cinderella dancing at the ball
Hansel and Gretel
Hansel and Gretel walking on the path
The lion, the witch, and the wardrobe
The lion, the witch, and the wardrobe together again
The enchanted forest
The enchanted forest at dusk
The enchanted forest at dusk as the rain falls
The troll
Hands clenched, the troll
The giant
The giant, the one who hoarded the bag of gold
Falling
Falling from the sky all day long
To howl like a wounded lion
In the middle of the night
Hiding in the middle of the night
To see easily
To see and to talk to the elf

The ogre that dug the cave

Crawling through the dank tunnel

Because the hero trounced the villain

Since the rain fell

As the enchanted horses galloped

Through the woods, over the hills, and into the night

Since she felt so alone

Although the giant loved gold

Which the evil queen hated the most

If the rain falls in a deluge

So much depends upon

The door opening slowly and mysteriously, like an ancient wooden eyelid

The cave having been dark

Sentence Subjects

The subject is the topic of the sentence. The subject may be a word, a phrase, or a clause. In the following sentences, the subjects are in italics.

Jack is climbing the beanstalk.

The boy climbing the beanstalk is Jack.

The door flew open.

To prowl the forest is the wolf's favorite activity.

Her dark, gray, wicked eyes stared at the sleeping figure.

That Sleeping Beauty didn't need sleeping pills is clear.

Sentence Predicates

The predicate tells what the subject is doing or what condition it is in. The predicate may be a word or a group of words. In the following sentences, the predicates are in italics.

Jack *is climbing* up the beanstalk.

The wolf *howled* at the moon.

Her eyes *closed*.

The ogre *rampaged* through the night.

Since the night of the royal ball, Cinderella *has received* a thousand invitations to go dancing.

Because the enchanted frog was kissed by the princess, he *ordered* all new clothes.

Sentence Activity I

Which of the following are sentences and which are not?

1. Elves talking among themselves.
2. The troll drenched with river water.
3. In the dark cave, the dragon sleeping and snoring.
4. The wolf donned grandma's clothes and beckoned Little Red Riding Hood.
5. The frogs, the crows, and the mice.
6. Briar Rose wept.
7. Cinderella was so happy.
8. Odysseus hid in the belly of a horse.
9. The other Greek warriors hunched in the belly of the horse.
10. Because she was envious of Sleeping Beauty.
11. Jack, the boy who climbed the beanstalk and nabbed the gold.
12. Trembling like a leaf in a cool breeze, Gretel alone in the house.
13. Instead of gobbling the ripe, red apple.
14. Stop.
15. Gone.
16. Sweet.
17. Speak.
18. Cool.
19. Happy is the ogre who spends his days in the dark.
20. The last time the Frog Prince.

Sentence Activity II

Turn the following fragments into sentences; you will need to add a subject or a predicate.

1. In the bottom of the slimy well, _____.
2. _____ ran into the castle and called for help.
3. The troll _____.
4. Conjuring a magic spell, _____.
5. Eyes wide, hands clenched, _____.
6. The day having been bright, _____.
7. _____ is the worst thing that could have happened to Jack.
8. Because she had to bolt at midnight, _____.
9. Her hair dangling out the window, _____.
10. The third pig _____.

Compound Subjects and Predicates

Both subjects and predicates can be compounds; that means that more than one of each of them can appear in a sentence.

If a sentence has a compound subject it contains two or more subjects; the subjects are tied together by the words *and, or,* or *nor.* Compound subjects share the same verb (in the predicate). The following sentences contain compound subjects.

> *The elf* and *the wizard* were hitchhiking to Oz.
>
> Either *Sleeping Beauty* or *Briar Rose* ordered the magic pizza.
>
> *Sleeping in trees* and *lounging in meadows* are two of Rip Van Winkle's favorite things.
>
> *The giant's bellow* and *its echo* lasted for nine days.
>
> *To ride in an expensive coach* and *to dance at the royal ball* were two things that Cinderella wanted most in life.

If a sentence has a compound predicate, it contains two or more main verbs; the predicates are tied together by the words *and, or,* or *nor.* Compound predicates share the same subject. The following sentences contain compound predicates.

> Rapunzel *looked* out the window and *unfurled* her long hair.
>
> Goldilocks *entered* the bear's house, *ate* some porridge, and *shattered* a small chair.
>
> The wolf's protestations neither *convinced* the judge nor *placated* the wounded pig.
>
> The blackbird *led* the distraught mother through the forest and *delivered* her to Heckedy Peg's door.

Writing Activity

Add a compound predicate to each of the following:

1. The maladroit queen _____.
2. Since he was lost and alone, Jack _____.
3. Singing a sweet song and skipping through the forest, Briar Rose _____
   _____.
4. Suddenly the giant _____.
5. The bats, those strange creatures who fly at night, _____.
6. Envious of the prince's good fortune, the thief _____.
7. To display her disapproval, Cinderella's stepmother _____
   _____.
8. The hermit _____.
9. Riding on a magic carpet, the genie _____.
10. Toward the end of his journey, the woodsman _____.

Add a compound subject to each of the following:

1. _____
   were alone in the dungeon.

2. _____
   opened the book and held their breath.

3. _____
   smiled widely.

4. _____
   readied themselves for their long trip.

5. _____
   fluttered their eyelashes.

6. _____
   tugged the rope.

7. _____
   moped and moped and moped.

8. _____
   began to dance.

9. Whirling and twirling, _____
   shouted with glee.

10. To discover the secret route, _____
    unfolded the map.

Direct Object

A direct object is a word or group of words that follow a verb and answer the question *what?* or *whom?*

The elf ate *a pear.*
The dragon burned *everything.*
The king decided *the matter.*
The king decided *to show that he was the boss.*
The king decided *that living in a damp castle was not a good idea.*
The frog found *it.*
The wolf surprised *her.*
Frogs love *swimming.*
The troll hurled *the boulder.*

Indirect Object

An indirect object is a word or group of words that follow a verb and tell *to* or *for whom* or *what*.

The witch gave *Snow White* a poisoned apple.

Jack's mother sent *him* a belated birthday card.

Dorothy showed *the witch* her new ruby slippers.

Predicate Noun

A predicate noun follows a linking verb; it gives information about or identifies the subject of the sentence.

The story is a *tragedy*.

The stepmother was a *spy*.

His happiness was her *grief*.

The creature is a *unicorn*.

The creature was a *biped*.

Predicate Adjective

A predicate adjective follows a linking verb; it gives information about the subject of the sentence.

The troll's tea was *harsh*.

The witch's teeth are *jagged*.

After his ordeal, Jack looked *terrible*.

Because she took a bite of the apple, Snow White became *weary*.

The giant sounds *angry*.

The elf is *magical*.

Achilles seemed *distracted*.

During the cold night, the birds remained *inactive*.

Normally, predicate adjectives following the linking verb, to be: am, are, is, was, were, been, will be, has been, will have been, could be, would be. Predicate adjectives also follow look, hear, taste, smell, sound, and other verbs such as appear, seem, become, grown, prove, remain.

Parallel Structure in Sentences

A parallel structure in a sentence is a group of words or phrases that are structured in the same way.

> Incorrect: Cinderella loves dancing, singing, and to ride in carriages. (The two participles and the infinitive are not parallel.)
> Correct: Cinderella loves dancing, singing, riding in carriages.
>
> Incorrect: Rapunzel is kind, caring, and has a sly personality. (The clause does not parallel the two adjectives that precede it.)
> Correct: Rapunzel is kind, caring, and sly.
>
> Incorrect: Either the ogre will knock down the bridge or the giant had schemed to find a new magical harp. (The verbs before and after the conjunction must be the same tense.)
> Correct: Either the ogre will knock down the bridge or the giant will scheme to find a new magical harp.

Sentence Structures

1. **Simple:** a sentence that contains one subject and one predicate.

   Rumpelstiltskin refused to give his name.
   Jack grabbed the bag of gold.
   Snow White is asleep.

2. **Compound:** a sentence that contains two or more subjects and two or more predicates.

   Jack and Rapunzel are cousins. (two subjects)
   Jack grabbed the gold and slid down the beanstalk. (two predicates)

   Two independent clauses that are joined with conjunctions are compound sentences:
   Rumpelstiltskin tried to trick the queen, but his trick backfired.
   The book was open, but its pages were unreadable.
   The dragon kicked down the door, and he was not happy.

3. **Complex:** a sentence that has an independent clause and a dependent clause:

   The giant *who looks for beanstalks* often finds them. (dependent clause)
   If a beanstalk grows, Jack will climb it. (dependent clause)
   While Snow White slept, the dwarfs played poker. (dependent clause)

4. **Compound-complex:** a sentence that has two (or more) independent clauses and one dependent clause.

   The giant who looks for beanstalks often finds them, but he thinks of them only as weeds.
   If a beanstalk grows, Jack will climb it because he loves high places.
   While Snow White slept, the dwarfs played poker, but they played quietly.

Ten Sentence Patterns to Imitate

Here are ten expanded sentence patterns. Using them as models, create your own.

1. **A sentence that has two clauses connected with a semicolon:**

   Rapunzel escaped from her tower; the witch wept and yelled.

   Jack grabbed the hen and bag of gold; the giant growled and grumbled.

   Blackbirds gathered overhead; Cinderella's sisters got nervous.

   The ogres laughed; the sprites trembled.

2. **A sentence that joins two clauses with a colon (in this pattern, the clause that comes after the colon will explain a word or idea in the first clause):**

   The missing hen, harp, and bag of gold could only mean one thing: Jack had been in the house.

   Vasalisa never forgot her mother's last words: "Stay out of the forest."

   There is one important thing to remember about small trolls: they don't like being called trollettes.

   Little Red Riding Hood learned an important lesson: wolves like to dress up in women's clothing.

3. **A sentence that contains a series of words that are separated by commas:**

   Achilles was rude, abrasive, and petulant.

   With courage, patience, and fortitude, Rapunzel overcame many difficulties.

   Wringing her hands, stamping her feet, and twitching her ears, the mama troll called for her lost children.

4. **A sentence that contains groups of words that are connected by conjunctions:**

   Rapunzel and Cinderella, Snow White and Briar Rose, Red Riding Hood and Vasalisa are all famous folktale heroines.

   The story of the Odyssey is one of love and betrayal, hope and despair, courage and cowardice, wisdom and foolishness, honor and deception.

   Jack knew the differences between giants and ogres, elves and dwarfs, witches and wizards.

5. **A series of words that give more information about the subject of the sentence; these words are separated from the rest of the sentence by dashes.**

   The essential qualities of a hero—courage, selflessness, and honor—Jack learned the hard way.

   The ogre was upset because his favorite foods—mud pie, burnt corn on the cob, and worm stew—were no longer on the menu of his favorite cafe.

   The chief villains in folktales—witches, giants, trolls, and ogres—are not mean; they are really just misunderstood.

6. **A series of clauses, joined by commas, at the beginning of the sentence:**

   If you hear a ghostly howl, if you feel the temperature suddenly drop, if you feel your skin begin to crawl, you know the banshee is near.

   Whether you are lost in a dark forest, whether you are adrift in a stormy sea, whether you are locked in a castle dungeon, you need magic to get find your way home.

   When the mirror cracks, when the witch cackles, run for your life.

7. **A sentence that repeats and expands on a word and is separated from the rest of the sentence:**

The witch held up an apple—an apple dripping with poison.

Folktales present characters from a strange world—the world of the imagination.

The dwarfs witnessed her terrible laugh—a laugh that, earlier in the day, had been sweet and clear.

8. **Sentences that contain contrasts (this, not that):**

Some people say that Jack was lucky, not brave.

Vasalisa stepped fearfully through a dark forest, not an arid desert.

The troll hid beneath a bridge, not a bunker.

Elves, not ogres, are gentle forest folk.

The giant demanded vengeance, not justice.

9. **Two predicates (and phrases) joined by a conjunction in a question:**

Would you rather race a wolf or arm-wrestle a giant?

Would you rather go to the ball with Cinderella or descend into a dungeon with Trog the Troll?

Would you rather drink moonbeam tea and eat angelhair pasta or slurp slug pie and gobble sour pumpkin bread?

Would you rather be a wolf in sheep's clothing or a sheep in wolf's clothing?

10. **Short sentences that create emphasis.**

Stop thief!

The mirror shattered.

The giant belched.

The earth rumbled.

Crows cawed.

Her face fell.

Sentence Imitation

Here are ten sentences to imitate. Write a sentence like each of the following; keep the same structure, but change the content.

1. **Meandering through the meadow, Snow White discovered a magic wand.**

_____

_____

2. **After they had run for half a day, the trolls heaved a sigh of relief.**

_____

_____

3. **I am called Quark; I am leader of the elusive forest elves.**

_____

_____

4. Rapunzel, the girl with long, flowing hair, remained trapped in her tower for twenty years.

_____

_____

5. Briar Rose, who confessed her part in the great pie theft, was banished to the land of the ogres.

_____

_____

6. On this side of the forest, children happily play; on the other side of the forest, goblins lurk by night.

_____

_____

7. The frog prince dove into the well because he wished to retrieve the princess's golden orb.

_____

_____

8. Justice, justice, justice—the giant demanded justice.

_____

_____

9. Instead of silk, the troll wore burlap; instead of cashmere, the troll wore cardboard; and instead of wool, the troll wore sandpaper.

_____

_____

10. The dragon, famished and weary, arrived at sunset, settled in the town square, and demanded a cartload of roasted ham.

_____

_____

Find other sentences in books you are reading and imitate them.

Sixteen Kinds of Sentences: Different Constructions for Different Purposes

Each of the following sentences is designed to achieve a specific purpose. For that reason, each sentence has a unique structure.

1. **Generalization:** All frogs are beautiful.

2. **Summary:** To conclude, as you have seen, we can put folktale characters into three categories.

3. **Comparison:** The Wolf is more of a villain than the Troll.

4. **Contrast:** Cinderella was industrious, but Jack was indolent.

5. **Cause/Effect:** If Snow White eats the apple, she will plunge into a deep sleep.

6. **Opinion:** I think "The Three Pigs" is the greatest folktale ever told.

7. **Definition:** A villain is a scoundrel in a story or play.

8. **Procedure:** First, plant the beans. Second, water them. Third, wait. Fourth, once the beanstalk has shot into the sky, begin climbing.

9. **Problem/Solution:** Jack and his mother were poor until he absconded with the Giant's hen that laid golden eggs, the bag of gold, and the magical harp.

10. **Simile:** The dragon streaked through the sky like a wingéd comet with a bad attitude.

11. **Metaphor:** The story is a portal to a new world.

12. **Hyperbole:** The witch was meaner than a boxcar filled with hornets.

13. **Law/Principle:** Every time fairy-tale characters are told not to do something, they always ignore the order, do what they shouldn't, and find themselves in trouble.

14. **Catalogue of Facts:** The castle was filled with dukes and barons, princesses and duchesses, and jesters and jugglers.

15. **Assertion (with one general idea):** Scrooge was a greedy fellow.

16. **Transition (*transition word is in italics*):** *Another* problem that the Wolf had to overcome was his bad breath.

Writing Activity

Choose a topic. Write about it using the kinds of sentences that you are directed to use in each of the following.

EXAMPLE:

Create a sentence using these four patterns:

15 (assertion), 7 (definition), 5, (cause/effect), 6 (opinion)

King Midas was avaricious. By avaricious, I mean that he valued gold above everything else—he even valued gold above his love for his daughter. His avarice caused him to turn everything he touched—including his daughter—into gold. I think that, surrounded by nothing but gold, he became gold-lonely.

Try your own sentences using these patterns:

1. 4, 14, 3, 7

_____

_____

2. 15, 14, 13, 1

_____

_____

3. 9, 10, 14, 2

_____

_____

4. 8, 3, 6

_____

_____

Figurative Language

The following are devices that writers use to spice up and energize their writing. These are especially helpful when it comes to revision. Which of these do you notice in what you are reading? Which of these can you add to your writing to spice it up?

Repetition: the employment of words or phrases more than once to achieve emphasis in ideas and/or rhythm

> Beware, beware
> of the bear out there,
> Of the bear out there.
> The bear out there
> Likes to prowl and growl
> And paw the hair of hikers there.
> So beware, beware
> Of the bear out there.
>
> A snack, a snack,
> My kingdom
> For a snack!
>
> Fire, fire burning bright.
> Fire, fire a blazing sight.

Alliteration: the repetition of a beginning consonant or consonant sound

> Peter Piper picked a peck of pickled peppers.
> Betty Botter bought a batch of bitter butter.
> Red robins rise on wings in a ring.
> Daffodils dream of dancing on dew-dappled days.
> Rapunzel repelled reluctantly on a rough rope.

Onomatopoeia: the use of words that "sound like" the audio-images to which they refer

Bees murmur and buzz

Fireworks sizzle, crackle, zip, and pop

Waves crash and slap, roar, and roll

Simile: a comparison of two objects (one object must be concrete), using "like" or "as"

Water sprinkled on the hot griddle scattered like startled geese.

A rainbow is like a large box of crayons—stretched out.

A sun setting is like a gold coin dropped into a big vending machine on the other side of the earth.

Thunder sounds like a whale doing belly flops in the clouds.

Similes That Show: Abstract Ideas Made Concrete

Sadness: I felt like a pink flower on a foggy day the day my cat didn't come home.

Sadness: The night my dad left, I felt like a blackboard that had just been erased.

Embarrassment: When the teacher looked at my empty paper, I felt like a light bulb that just burned out.

Boredom: As I listened to him talk, I felt like I was on a flat and endless road in Kansas.

Metaphor: an analogy identifying one object with another and ascribing to the first object one or more qualities of the second

Our front lawn is our house's wide green moustache.

A mountain is an ice cream cone turned upside down.

A dream that is never fulfilled is a seed that dies in the ground.

Metaphors That Show: Abstract Ideas Made Concrete

Happiness: When I finished my homework, I felt bright yellow—I was all sun inside.

Confusion: When I got to the fifth-grade spelling bee, my brain was a deck of cards scattered and strewn across the floor.

Loneliness: I was a "Dead End" sign on a street where nobody lives.

Anger: The day my bike was stolen I felt a bull thrashing my stomach, trying to break out.

Personification: endowing animals, objects, or ideas with human qualities

When the sun goes home at day's end, it takes a shiny key from a ring of stars and unlocks the door of night.

From constantly spinning and blinking, the lighthouse grew dizzy.

The locked door envied the elevator.

When I turn it on, the light on my desk casts a wide smile while the candle I just blew out sends up a slow shiver of lonely smoke.

The thunder erupts
On huge tiger paws.

It roars raucously
Over roofs and tree-tops
With wide-spread jaws
And then pounces away.

Hyperbole: an exaggeration (often takes the form of simile or metaphor)

He took a breath bigger than a circus tent.
It was so cold that the house turned blue.
It was so cold that the chickens laid frozen eggs.
He had an alligator mouth.

A Note on Voice

■ What is *voice* in writing?

_____

■ Do you detect *different voices* in the following? Describe the voice in each one.

a. Shall we hasten to depart these premises?

_____

b. Hey! Let's go!

_____

c. Look, would you please come on, already? Aw, just come on, okay?

_____

d. I'm awfully sorry to bother you, but do you think, that maybe, we should go?

_____

Answers: a. (formal)   b. (informal, angry)   c. (whiny, pleading)   d. (timid, unsure)

■ Describe the voices in these two passages: (Notice that the speaker in each passage is talking about the same thing.)

a. "During the whole of a dull, dark, and soundless day in the autumn of the year, when the clouds hung oppressively low in the heavens, I had been passing alone on horseback through a singularly dreary tract of country . . ." (Poe, 1990, 691).

_____

_____

b. I was, like, riding this really radical horse, and it's name was, I think, Silver or Scout or something, and I was trotting through this totally trashed territory, you know, and the clouds—they were kinda gray and heavy like half-fat water balloons (Dude, I love water balloons!)—made me feel sort of sad, but then I thought, "Da, lighten up, 'cause I'm like a knight or a king riding this really radical horse," and I felt better, you know?

_____

_____

Answers: a. (a formal, somber voice from Edgar Allen Poe's, "The Fall of the House of Usher") b. (the casual, energetic voice of a "surfer-dude")

■ What is *voice* in writing?

While we may think of voice as the sound of a person speaking, voice in writing is a little different than that. We cannot actually "hear" a writer's voice because all we have are the writer's words (silent) on the page. Since we cannot "hear" a writer's voice with our ears, we have to hear the voice in our minds. We have to create a voice in our minds that best fits the ideas and the mood of the words on the page. Since all we have to work with are the writer's words, we can think of voice as this: Voice = the kinds of words the writer uses and the length of the sentences the writer creates. To say it another way:

VOICE = WORD CHOICE + SENTENCE LENGTH (structure)

A writer's voice may be: friendly, serious, distant, angry, cheerful, bitter, cynical, reverential, awe-struck, enthusiastic, morbid, resentful, warm, cold, remorseful, sad, playful, confused, curious, sarcastic, nostalgic, pleading, assertive, gloomy, longing, etc.

By carefully choosing the right words (parts of speech) and the right sentence length (combinations of phrases and clauses), writers create the voices that best fit what they are writing about.

Notice how the words and length of the sentences create voice:

Oh, one day my prince will come and free me from languishing in this lonely tower. (longing)

Why do I always get stuck with the lousy jobs. (resentful)

Sure, sure, Mr. Ogre, oh, you are definitely an extremely handsome creature. (sarcastic)

I remember the days when life was good, when the summer days were warm, when songbirds filled the air with sweet melodies. (nostalgic)

Notice how changing a few words creates a different voice:

The gnome sauntered down the quiet street.

The gnome frantically dashed down the street that was lined with hungry dragons.

The first sentence has a quiet, relaxed voice. The second has an energetic voice that is edged with fear and danger.

Voice Works

Using the "right" parts of speech and the "right" phrases and clauses:

1. **Write a sentence that has a happy voice:** (Think of a character from something you have read who has made a happy discovery. What would he or she say? Pay careful attention to word choice and sentence length.)

    _____

    _____

2. **Write a sentence that has a sad voice:** (Think of a character from something you have read who is feeling sad. Why would he or she be sad? What has made him or her sad? Pay careful attention to word choice and sentence length.)

    _____

    _____

3. **Write a sentence that has an angry voice:** (Think of a character from something you have read who is feeling angry. Why would he or she be angry? What has made him or her angry? Pay careful attention to word choice and sentence length.)

    _____

    _____

4. **Write a sentence that has a frightened voice:** (Think of a character from something you have read who is feeling afraid. What would he or she say? Why would he or she say it? Why would he or she be frightened? Pay careful attention to word choice and sentence length.)

    _____

    _____

5. **Write a sentence that has a curious voice:** (Think of a character from something you have read who is feeling curious. What would he or she say? Why would he or she say it? What has made him or her curious? Pay careful attention to word choice and sentence length.)

    _____

    _____

Word Play

Words are like little winged creatures flitting into our ears and out of our mouths. They can buzz with sudden intensity, drone with sleepy languor, hover just out of reach, or even sting with precise barbs.

Words assume various shapes and shape us in various ways. They can constellate into a poem, a story, a play, an essay, a novel, a scientific report, a math-story problem, a letter, a text message, a textbook, a list of ingredients on a cereal box, a riddle, a joke. . . . By their very nature, words are flexible, pliable, fluid, flexible, playful. They can create many moods—sad or glad, somber or soulful, bizarre or nostalgic, mad or happy, wistful or doleful, breezy or dreadful—in different kinds of writing. As such, and being the only tools that writers have, words offer endless possibilities of meaning—if writers know how to approach them.

For both the developing and the established writer, the "right"—or "write"—way to approach words is through play. When writers play with words, they must adopt and employ an attitude that is open, hopeful, receptive, and flexible. To be successful, writers must combine their experience with their knowledge of what words can do; they must make a relationship to language, one that is respectful and undemanding.

When writers play with words, words play with them. Which is to say, to play with words is to become open to the possibilities that words offer. And the more open we are, the more surprises and connections words will offer. It's as if words know when writers are open and playful and when they are not.

Consider, for example, some of the poets who write for young writers. Writers such as Shel Silverstein, Jack Prelutsky, Bill Martin Jr., Karla Kushkin, and Judith Viorst (to name but a few), write from and with a playful perspective. Consequently, their poems tend to be lively and enlivening, delightful and engaging, immediate and lingering.

The activities in this section are designed to help young writers learn how to make meaning—sometimes serious, often silly—by playing with language. In doing so, they may uncover many ways to communicate their intended ideas, and even discover new ones. Through word play, young authors will develop flexible thinking (the ability to see new ideas and new situations, to see from a fresh perspective). They may also find unique ways to enter into an ongoing and happy relationship with words and with the ideas that words can carry and convey.

Answers for each section can be found at the end of the chapter.

Word Building I

How many words can you make from combinations of the following letters?

a e e i l r r t t u

EXAMPLES:

rail	trail	true
tree	late	rattle

Now you try:

_____ _____ _____

_____ _____ _____

Put all the letters together to create one large word.

_____

Word Building II

How many words can you make from combinations of the following letters?

a e l n p r u z

_____ _____ _____

_____ _____ _____

Put all the letters together to create one large word.

_____

Word Building III

How many words can you make from combinations of the following letters?

a c d e e i l l n r

_____ _____ _____

_____ _____ _____

Put all the letters together to create one large word.

_____

Word Building IV

How many words can you make from combinations of the following letters?

a b b d g f i l o w

_____ _____ _____

_____ _____ _____

Put all the letters together to create one large word.

_____

Word Building V

How many words can you make from combinations of the following letters?

e i i k l l m n p r s s t t u

_____ _____ _____

_____ _____ _____

Put all the letters together to create three words.

_____

Add-a-Letter

Start with a letter and keep adding one letter at a time until you have made as many words as possible.

EXAMPLE:

a
at
sat
spat
splat (or spate)

Try building words from these:

i	a	t
p	g	n
o	h	m

Change-a-Letter

How many new words can you create by changing just one letter in the target word?

EXAMPLE:

Target word 1: home

New words made by changing just one letter in the word *home*:

tome	some	hose
hope	hone	hole
dome	come	Rome

Target word 2: game

Create new words by changing one letter:

_____   _____   _____

_____   _____   _____

_____   _____   _____

Target word 3: lake

Create new words by changing one letter:

_____   _____   _____

_____   _____   _____

_____   _____   _____

Target word 4: hole

Create new words by changing one letter:

_____   _____   _____

_____   _____   _____

_____   _____   _____

Collecting Collective Nouns

Groups of animals are usually referred to with special nouns called COLLECTIVE NOUNS. For instance, a group of lions is called a "pride"; a group of geese is called a "gaggle"; a group of doves is called a "bevy"; a group of fish is called a "school"; a group of rhinoceroses is called a "crash"; and a group of owls is called a "parliament."

Some groups, however, don't have official collective nouns. Can you create collective nouns for the following groups? For example, a group of plumbers might be called "a plunger of plumbers"; and a group of race-car drivers might be called "a hubcap of race car drivers."

teachers	clowns	lawyers
doctors	actors	students
archaeologists	astronauts	musicians
bakers	piano movers	farmers
zookeepers	veterinarians	bankers
grocery baggers	electricians	salespersons

Multiple-Meaning Words

Some words have many meanings. How many different meanings can you think of for the following words?

set	plant	bank
bend	see	show
blast	present	size

How many other multiple-meaning words can you think of?

Synonyms

How many synonyms can you think of for the following words?

EXAMPLE:

Walk: ambulate, foot (it), hoof, pace, step, traipse, tread, troop, amble, circumambulate, mosey, perambulate, promenade, ramble, saunter, stroll, hike, tramp, trek, lumber, plod, slog, stride, stump, trudge, leg, race, run, beat one's feet, heel

Happy: _____

Sad: _____

Crazy: _____

Angry: _____

Run: _____

Write: _____

Say: _____

What's in a Word?

Can you guess the correct definition for each of the following words?

eggler

a. a cup for holding an egg that is to be eaten from the shell

b. an egg-dealer of the 1700s in Scotland

c. a carved ornamental design consisting of an egg-shaped figure alternating with a figure somewhat like an elongated javelin or arrowhead

d. a drink consisting of whipped eggs, milk, a flavoring syrup, and soda water

pismire

a. last resource or device; expedient

b. a common ant (used by Chaucer in *The Canterbury Tales*)

c. of, relating to, or dependent on fish or fishing

d. a meal of fish and small waterfowl

Find five unusual words in the dictionary; write down the correct definition of each and make up three false definitions that sound realistic for each. Share your words and definitions with your classmates; ask them to guess which of your definitions is correct.

Word Spectrum

Put the words in each group in order of degree, from *least* to *most*.

Group One

frigid   cool   cold   freezing

chilly   brisk   glacial   frosty

Group Two

warm   fiery   tropical   sizzling

sultry   blistering   tepid   sweltering

Group Three

mean   spiteful   ornery   baneful

vile   repulsive   malignant   malevolent

Very Special Paragraphs

Do you notice anything special about these paragraphs?

Up to about its primary school days a child thinks, naturally, only of play. But many a form of play contains disciplinary factors. "You can't do this," or "that puts you out" shows a child that it must think practically or fail. Now, if, throughout childhood, a brain has no opposition, it is plain that it will attain a position of "status quo," as with our ordinary animals. Man knows not why a cow, dog or lion was not born with a brain on a par with ours; why such animals cannot add, subtract, or obtain from books and schooling, that paramount position which Man holds today.

But a human brain is not in that class. Constantly throbbing and pulsating, it rapidly forms opinions; attaining an ability of its own; a fact which is startlingly shown by an occasional child "prodigy" in music or school work. And as, with our dumb animals, a child's inability convincingly to impart its thoughts to us should not class it as ignorant. (Wright 1939)

What did you notice?

Lipograms

These paragraphs can be found in a book entitled, *Gadsby: A Story of over 50,000 Words without the Letter "E"* written by Ernest Vincent Wright. Wright typed the entire manuscript the this story with the letter *E* tied down so that he was not able to use it as he wrote. Writing that purposefully excludes particular letters is called a *lipogram*.

Activity

Write about yourself in the lipogram mode. In other words, write about something you've done, someone you've met, some place you've been, or something you can do, but leave out one of these letters: *a, e, i, o,* or *u*. (If you really want a challenge, leave out the letter *e* as Wright did; *e* is the most commonly used vowel in the English language.)

First, write about yourself without leaving any letters out. Then revise your writing by dropping one letter (and by choosing new words to put in place of the words you had to drop because they contained your target letter). Have fun with your *lipogram*!

Try rewriting the following using the lipogram method:

Rewrite "Humpty Dumpty" without using the letter *A*.

Humpty Dumpty sat on the wall,
Humpty Dumpty had a great fall.
All the king's horses,
And all the king's men
Couldn't put Humpty together again.

Rewrite "Jack Sprat" without using the letter *T*.

Jack Sprat could eat no fat,
His wife could eat no lean.
And so between them both, you see,
They licked the platter clean.

Rewrite "Hickory, Dickory" without using the letter *O*.

Hickory, dickory, dock,
The mouse ran up the clock.
The clock struck one,
The mouse ran down,
Hickory, dickory, dock.

Rewrite "Polly" without using the letter *T*.

Polly put the kettle on,
Polly put the kettle on,
Polly put the kettle on,
We'll all have some tea.

Concrete Poetry

These poems are made of words that show the shapes of the objects they are describing. For example: "Christmas Tree":

                        A
                        Fir
                        tree
                        makes
                        a great
                        Christmas
                            t
                            r
                            e
                            e

Arrow

            t
                h
                    e
    I always hit   m
                a
            r
        k

Think of a shape that could be made out of words. Try creating your own concrete poem.

Word Connections

Think of colors, adjectives, and verbs that go with the following nouns.

Example: frog

colors	*adjectives*	*verbs*
green	fast	leap
blue	mysterious	croak
red	slick	spring
yellow	dangerous	flick
gold	wide-mouthed	plop
grey	stealthy	swim

Make word connections with these nouns:

cat	snake	bat
car	balloon	comet
bear	dog	horse
fish	bug	sloth

Try using as many words as you can (from your lists) in a sentence or a poem about one of the nouns (you can add words that are not in your lists if you choose).

EXAMPLE:

Frog
fast, furious, stealthy—
green leaps, plops in ponds,
blue darts from tree-to-tree in soggy rain forests,
gold hides and chirps in
    distant South American mountains,
yellow rises with the sun—

Words and Sounds

Choose an answer to each question and offer reasons to explain why.

1. **Which is louder?**

   crash or plop   _____

   ping or smash   _____

   bang or blip   _____

   buzz or hiss   _____

   roar or whisper   _____

   honk or zip   _____

2. **Which is harder?**

clatter or drip _____

splash or crunch _____

3. **Which is softer?**

fizz or click _____

rip or squish _____

4. **Which sounds could you hear in the city?**

beep	boom	caw	croak	roar
squeal	honk	bong	cluck	chirp

_____

5. **Which sounds could you hear in a school?**

buzz	ping	rattle	cheep	woosh
murmur	flutter	rip	chatter	grind
ring	hum			

_____

6. **Which sounds could you hear in the desert?**

quack	splash	twang	screech	tick tock
zip	cluck	honk	fizz	rustle
whirr	pop	hiss	flutter	buzz

_____

Riddles

To write riddles, follow these steps.

1. **Choose a topic: frogs (or bears, or pigs, or cows, etc.)**

2. **Make a list of words that you associate with the word *frog*.**

green	slimy	wart	hop
croak	legs	webs	lily pad
fly	tongue	leap	jump

3. **Choose one or two monosyllabic words from your list and drop the first letter (or blend).**

wart	hop
(w)art	(h)op

4. **List words that begin with the remaining letters.**

artichoke	article	artifact
opera	optimistic	opportunity
operation	open	optometrist

5. **Put the dropped letter from step "c" onto the words from step "d." Put a "w" onto the words that begin with "art"; put an "h" onto the words that begin with "op."**

6. Now you have answers to frog riddles; choose one and write a question that goes with it.

Question: Why did the frog go to the hospital?
Answer: He needed a hoperation.

Question: What does a frog journalist write?
Answer: He writes warticles.

Rewritten Titles

Can you figure out the titles of these books?

1. The locale of untamed creatures (*Where the Wild Things Are*)

2. Perambulate for a pair or lunar cycles

   _____

3. Engage in hostile conflict with cocoa bean and sugar

   _____

4. One who bestows

   _____

5. A short-handled ax often with a hammerhead to be used with one hand

   _____

6. Furtive things of an urban area featuring a variety of shops surrounding a usually open-air concourse reserved for pedestrian traffic

   _____

7. A smooth-skinned, web-footed, largely aquatic, tailless, agile leaping amphibian and an amphibian that is generally more terrestrial in habit though returning to water to lay their eggs, squatter and shorter in build and with weaker hind limbs, and rough, dry, and warty rather than smooth and moist of skin

   _____

8. Hollowed-out places

   _____

9. A post-sunset farewell to the lunar object

   _____

10. A huge number of carnivorous mammals long domesticated as pets and for catching rats and mice

    _____

11. A stunning slumberer

    _____

12. A trio of brusque hollow-horned ruminant mammals

    _____

Can you figure out the titles of these nursery rhymes?

1. **Maternal game bird of advanced years**

   _____

2. **Irreparable, broken egg**

   _____

3. **Seated lass, fearful of dangling arachnids**

   _____

4. **Searching shepherd girl**

   _____

5. **Swift boy who leaps over flames**

   _____

6. **Musical feline and dancing dishes**

   _____

7. **Elderly woman with hungry dog and empty cabinets**

   _____

8. **Clumsy couple on an errand to a well**

   _____

9. **Elderly, happy monarch who smoked and ate plenty**

   _____

10. **Small boy who eats his pies with his hands**

    _____

11. **Elderly woman of sole**

    _____

12. **Tired shepherd boy with a trumpet**

    _____

Half a Proverb

Here are the first half of some proverbs and sayings; how will you complete them?

1. A stitch in time _____
2. Do unto others _____
3. Penny wise and _____
4. All's well that _____
5. The ends _____
6. Make hay while _____

7. Don't cry over _____

8. A bird in the hand _____

9. It is better to have _____

10. People who live in glass houses _____

11. A penny saved is _____

Good News, Bad News I

Complete the following writing pattern:

Good News: I just rowed into the ocean to go fishing.
Bad News: The boat sprung a leak.

Good News: Luckily I had a can of "leak-stopper."
Bad News: The can was empty.

Good News: _____

Bad News: _____

Good News: _____

Bad News: _____

Good News: _____

Bad News: _____

Good News: _____

Bad News: _____

Good News: _____

Bad News: _____

Good News: _____

Bad News: _____

Good News: _____

Bad News: _____

Good News: _____

Bad News: _____

Good News: _____

Bad News: _____

Good News: _____

Bad News: _____

Good News, Bad News II

Complete the following writing pattern:

Good News: I found a $100 bill on the street this morning.
Bad News: The bill wasn't real.

Good News: The fake bill had a lottery ticket attached to it.
Bad News: I couldn't read the numbers on the ticket.

Good News: _____

Bad News: _____

Good News: _____

Bad News: _____

Good News: _____

Bad News: _____

Good News: _____

Bad News: _____

Good News: _____

Bad News: _____

Good News: _____

Bad News: _____

Good News: _____

Bad News: _____

Good News: _____

Bad News: _____

Good News: _____

Bad News: _____

Writing Questions

- Think of people, animals, and objects that "do" things.
- Think of actions that these people, animals, and objects do.
- Create a question about a person, object, or animal based on what they do.
- Use the following pattern: person/animal/object plus action. Here are some examples.

Why does my brother always get away with things?

Why do dogs always bark just when I fall asleep?

Why do my parents make me eat broccoli?

Why do cats walk away when I want to pet them?

Why do doctors always make me say "ahh"?

Now try these:

Why does a baby _____ ?

Why do big kids _____ ?

Why does my best friend _____ ?

Flexible Thinking

1. **List all the things you can think of that come in pairs:**

2. **Tell all the ways an ant and a golf ball are alike:**

3. **Tell all the ways a cat and a refrigerator are alike:**

4. **What are your three favorite things? Why?**

5. **If you were a rainbow, tell three things you would think:**

6. **What are your three favorite words? Why? What are your three least favorite words? Why?**

7. **Here is the opening stanza from Lewis Carroll's "Jabberwocky":**

'Twas brillig, and the slithy toves
    Did gyre and gimble in the wabe:
All mimsy were the borogoves,
    And the mome raths outgrabe.

Try your hand at writing something where you include made-up words. Here's a pattern to get you started:

It was _____ in the afternoon, and the _____ in the air.

Suddenly, a _____ came crashing in while the _____ looked up

and _____ across the _____ .

Decision Making

Before starting a folktale unit, answer the following questions. Give reasons for your answers.

1. Would you rather be a wizard or a gremlin?

   _____

2. Would you rather meet a knight or a troll?

   _____

3. Would you rather take a trip with a dwarf or an elf?

   _____

4. Would you rather go shopping with a princess or a witch?

   _____

5. Would you rather try to rescue a troll in a hole with a goblin or a giant?

   _____

6. Would you rather hear a story from an ogre or a frog prince?

   _____

7. Who is stronger: a giant or an elf?

   _____

8. Who is kinder: a princess or a gremlin?

   _____

9. Who is more fun to play tag with: a frog prince or a dwarf?

   _____

10. Who is sillier: a troll or a wizard?

    _____

11. Who is better at finding things: a witch or a princess?

    _____

12. Who is braver: a knight or a troll?

    _____

13. Who would be the best friend: a wizard, a goblin, an ogre, or a giant?

    _____

14. Who would be the best one to help you with your homework: a knight, an elf, a troll, or a giant?

    _____

15. Give five ways that you are like one of the following: a wizard, a frog prince, a knight, a princess, an elf, or a giant.

    _____

More Decision Making

Imagine that you are leading a team of four explorers to the top of a mountain and to the dragon-sorcerer's castle. You job is to get three feathers from the dragon's wings. The dragon is fierce, nearly indestructible, and hates humans.

Decide what personality traits or emotional and mental characteristics the members of your team should possess. Choose them from the following:

able	blunt	lucky	open-minded	frantic
sensitive	courageous	trustworthy	nostalgic	angry
agreeable	giving	defeated	vivacious	thrilled
confident	gentle	inquisitive	selfish	intolerant
cranky	fragile	graceful	mysterious	mean
fierce	happy	secretive	tense	tender
determined	clever	athletic	persuasive	_____?

Choose three "explorers" from the list below; match each one with the words you chose from the list above.

Snow White	Big Bad Wolf	Jack
The Giant	Rumplestiltskin	Rapunzel
Sleeping Beauty	Frog Prince	Third Pig
The Troll	Red Riding Hood	Gretel
Mean Stepsister	Cinderella	Evil Queen

Rock 'n' Roll Names

We've probably all heard of the following rock 'n' roll bands:

> The Beatles
> The Rolling Stones
> Fleetwood Mac
> The Monkeys

Can you think of new names for rock 'n' roll bands using characters, settings, objects, and titles from books? For example:

> *Max and the Wild Things*
> *The Poisoned Apples*
> *The Toad-Frogs*
> *The Gold'n Straw Spinners*
> *The Sorcerer's Stones*

Revising Weak Sentences

Rewrite these sentences so that they are more vivid and more specific. Show the reader what is happening in them; paint pictures with words by using concrete language, phrases, and clauses.

EXAMPLE:

1. **Going down his street one day, he found something.**

   Sauntering down the path as the sun crested the sky, the ogre spied a shiny key hidden in the weeds.

   Scurrying down the slick street in the dead of night, Jack stumbled over a sack.

2. **We went through the woods and we saw some things.** _____
3. **The creature went into the water.** _____
4. **We heard a sound and we reacted.** _____
5. **The person was angry.** _____
6. **He felt sad.** _____
7. **She was happy.** _____
8. **They were confused.** _____
9. **The boy was bored.** _____
10. **The animal was hungry.** _____

Parts of Speech Review

Add up the parts of speech in each of the following sentences. Nouns = 5 cents; verbs (and verbals: infinitives, gerunds, and participles) = 10 cents; adjectives = 3 cents; adverbs = 4 cents; prepositions = 2 cents; conjunctions = 2 cents

1. The wolf eyes the pigs.   3 5 10 3 5 = 26 cents
2. The pig cowered behind the straw door. _____
3. Snow White bit deeply into the glistening apple. _____
4. Snow White is asleep. _____
5. From the clouds came the sound of rolling thunder. _____
6. To show his courage, Achilles challenged the entire army of Troy. _____
7. Either Achilles wins the battle, or the Greeks turn around and go home.

   _____
8. Suddenly, the door opened and a withered hand emerged. _____
9. Because the hand was so withered and emaciated, the dwarf screamed. _____
10. "Yikes!" exclaimed the tiny man as he finished turning the room of straw into golden thread. _____
11. Son biglaws flibber et son rabbarish. (nonsense words: what parts of speech are they?)

    _____
12. Ut lo sporrish, son berrger clubbos a sparkend en delo torrium. _____

Write three sentences: one worth 30 cents, one worth 40 cents, and one worth 55 cents.

Re-Arrangements I

Can you decipher these? The way the words, letters, and/or numbers are arranged suggests their meanings. For instance, the words in the top-right box mean "overworked and underpaid."

1 (with white oval)	<u>worked</u> paid	whirl (diagonal)
hacatt	s t o n e	worl....

Re-Arrangements II

Can you decipher these?

w
  a
    t
      e
        r
	way	me
		  a l
		me me
		a l a l

gl a s s ?	decision	_igh_

Re-Arrangements III
Can you decipher these?

switch	bbbbbbbbbbbbb bbbbbbbbbbbbbb bbbbbbbbbbbbbb bbbbbbbbbbbbbb bbbbbbbbbbbbbb bbbbbbbbbbbbbb	D N A H
world	esruoc	_ _ok _ _ok

Re-Arrangements IV
Can you decipher these?

stairs	storystorystory storystorystory storystorystory storystorystory storystorystory	**TOP** circus
ank**l**e	twin twin	reception

Re-Arrangements V
Can you decipher these?

King of Tabbies **Queen of Calicos** **King of Beagles** **Queen of Collies**	look kool	⊚ DOM
Hit	lo **head** ve **heels**	**drawer**

Re-Arrangements VI
Can you decipher these?

"**I**'**M**"	**moon**	*Tistitchme*
genius | madness	smile	**Whip**

Re-Arrangements VII
Can you decipher these?

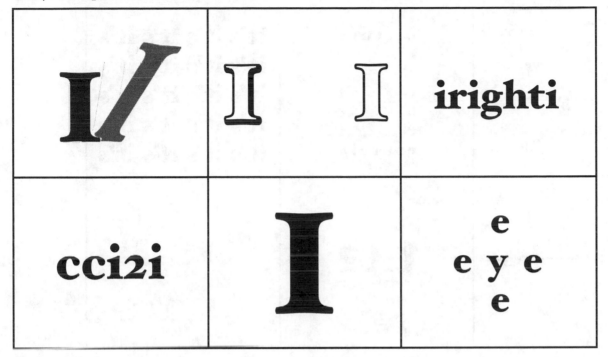

I✓	I I	irighti
cci2i	I	e e y e e

Re-Arrangements VIII
Can you decipher these?

noon	s t m o h c a	**draft**
e e **n n** **d d**	town	ooooooooo o o o o o o o o ooooooooo

Re-Arrangements IX

Can you decipher these?

n u s	picture / icture / cture / ture / erutcip (arranged around)	it's it's it's it's it's it's it's it's it's it's it's it's it's it's it's it's it's it's it's it's
~~tire~~	t42	pen

Re-Arrangements X

Can you decipher these?

L / -L / ̅O̅	times times	budget ∧
‾‾‾‾‾‾ / toe	carthorse	hour

Re-Arrangements XI
Can you decipher these?

bebreakfastd	r r r a t r a t r r	travel ccccccccccccc
G E S G	cheek *keehc*	h (a) o (l) u (l) s e

Re-Arrangements XII
Can you decipher these?

he's job	time time	e l t a t b a
[day] day	day day day *day*	**day**

Re-Arrangements XIII
Can you decipher these?

d l o h	passage	wolf
do e .	himselfhe's	mell w

Re-Arrangements XIV
Can you decipher these?

FIFTY STATE	COW	time
c h a n g e	BAD	pul led

Re-Arrangements XV
Can you decipher these?

c c c c c	**story**	→ story story story story story

whistling	ice	m
		  e
		    l
		      t

Answer Key

Word Building I:	"literature"
Word Building II:	"Rapunzel"
Word Building III:	"Cinderella"
Word Building IV:	"Big Bad Wolf"
Word Building V:	"Rumplestiltskin"

Change-a-Letter: words for "game": tame, same, name, lame, hame, gaze, gave, gate, gape, gamy, gale, fame, dame, came

words for "lake": wake, take, sake, rake, make, like, laze, lave, late, lane, lame, lade, lace, hake, fake, cake, bake

words for "hole": vole, sole, role, pole, mole, hove, hose, hope, hone, home, holy, hold, hale, dole, cole, bole

What's in a Word: eggler: correct answer is "b"
pismire: correct answer is "b"

Rewritten Titles

Books
2. *Walk Two Moons*
3. *The Chocolate War*
4. *The Giver*
5. *Hatchet*
6. *The Secrets of the Shopping Mall*
7. *Frog and Toad*
8. *Holes*
9. *Goodnight Moon*
10. *Millions of Cats*
11. *Sleeping Beauty*
12. *Three Billy Goats Gruff*

Nursery Rhymes
1. "Mother Goose"
2. "Humpty Dumpty"
3. "Little Miss Muffet"
4. "Little Bo Peep"
5. "Jack Be Nimble"
6. "Hey Diddle Diddle"
7. "Old Mother Hubbard"
8. "Jack and Jill"
9. "Old King Cole"
10. "Little Jack Horner"
11. "Old Woman in a Shoe"
12. "Little Boy Blue"

Half a Proverb:
1. A stitch in time saves nine.
2. Do unto others as you would have them do unto you.
3. Penny wise and pound foolish.
4. All's well that ends well.
5. The ends justify the means.
6. Make hay while the sun shines.
7. Don't cry over spilt milk.
8. A bird in the hand is worth two in the bush.
9. It is better to have loved and lost than never to have loved at all.
10. People who live in glass houses should not throw stones.
11. A penny saved is a penny earned.

Re-Arrangements

I: hole in one — overworked and underpaid
Tilt-a-Whirl — *The Cat in the Hat* — cornerstone — world without end

II: waterfall — highway — three square meals
Is the glass half full or half empty? — split decision
the middle of the night

III: light switch — a swarm of bees — handstand
the world on a string — reverse course — bookends

IV: the dark at the top of the stairs — never-ending story
big top over the circus — swollen ankle
identical twins — faint reception

V: raining cats and dogs — look both ways — dominos
pinch hit — head over heels in love — top drawer

VI: "I'm all shook up!" — full moon — a stitch in time
a fine line separating genius from madness
a faint smile — crack the whip

VII: eye shadow — eyes wide open
right between the eyes — to see eye to eye
big black eye — cross-eyes

VIII: high noon — upset stomach — rough draft
split ends — small town — ozone

IX: sunrise — picture frame — it's all over
flat tire — tea for two — penlight

X: noel — the best of times, the worst of times
balanced budget — undertow
putting the cart before the horse — half an hour

XI: breakfast in bed — double-crossing rat
travel overseas — scrambled eggs
turn the other cheek — all throughout the house

XII: he's on the job — time after time — uphill battle
day in, day out — strange days — daylight

XIII: hold up — narrow passage — big bad wolf
Dewey decimal — he's beside himself — mellow out

XIV: fifty state capitals — holy cow — time out
loose change — pretty bad — pulled apart

XV: seaside — short story — top story
whistling in the dark — black ice — meltdown

Passages to Edit

Reading Closely and Carefully to Find and Fix Errors

Good writers are good readers. They not only know how to go about writing by choosing the right tools—sixteen elements of grammar—to create texts that communicate clearly, but they also read widely and carefully. When good writers read, they read with a critical eye: an eye that knows what to look for, an eye that spots inconsistencies, and an eye that makes discoveries.

The following passages invite students to become careful and critical readers and to apply what they know about grammar to the reading process. In this way, students will read not only to discern content, but to scout and repair errors in each text.

Can you find fourteen misspelled words in the following passage?

The Aunt and the Grasshopper

In a feld one summer's day a Grasshopper was hoping about, chirping and singing to its hart's content. An Aunt passed by, baring along with great toil an ear of corn he was taking to the nist.

"Why not come and chatt with me," said the Grasshopper, "instead of toiling and moiling in that way?"

"I am helping to lay up food for the wenter," said the Aunt, "and recomend you to do the same."

"Why bother about wenter?" said the Grasshopper; we have got plenty of food at present." But the Ant went on its way and continued its toil. When the wenter came the Grasshopper had no food and found itself dieing of hunger, while it saw the ants distributing every day corn and grain from the stores they had colected in the summer. Then the Grasshopper knew:

It is best to prepare for the days of necesity.

Correctly spelled words in the corrected version below are in **bold print**.

The Ant and the Grasshopper (correct version)

In a **field** one summer's day a Grasshopper was **hopping** about, chirping and singing to its **heart's** content. An **Ant** passed by, **bearing** along with great toil an ear of corn he was taking to the **nest**.

"Why not come and **chat** with me," said the Grasshopper, "instead of toiling and moiling in that way?"

"I am helping to lay up food for the **winter**," said the **Ant**, "and **recommend** you to do the same."

"Why bother about **winter**?" said the Grasshopper; we have got plenty of food at present." But the Ant went on its way and continued its toil. When the **winter** came the Grasshopper had no food and found itself **dying** of hunger, while it saw the ants distributing every day corn and grain from the stores they had **collected** in the summer. Then the Grasshopper knew:

It is best to prepare for the days of **necessity**.

Can you find seven misspelled words in the following passage?

The Mule and the Frogs

A mulle, carrying a load of wood, passed thru a pond. As he was crossing thru the water he lost his footing, stummbled and fell, and not being able to rise on account of his load, groaned heavily. Some Frogs freqenting the pool herd his lamentation, and said, "What would you do if you had to live here always as we do, when you make such a fuss about a mere fall into the water?"

Men often bear little grievances with less curage than they do large misfortunes.

The Mule and the Frogs (correct version)

A **mule**, carrying a load of wood, passed **through** a pond. As he was crossing **through** the water he lost his footing, **stumbled** and fell, and not being able to rise on account of his load, groaned heavily. Some Frogs **frequenting** the pool **heard** his lamentation, and said, "What would you do if you had to live here always as we do, when you make such a fuss about a mere fall into the water?"

Men often bear little grievances with less **courage** than they do large misfortunes.

In the following passage some words shouldn't have double letters, but they do. Can you find them?

Avaricious and Envious

Two neighbors came before the king and asked him too grant their hearts' desire. Now, the one was full of avvarice, and the other eaten up with envvy. Soo to punish them both, the king granted that each might have whattever he wished for himself, but only onn the condition that his neighbor had twice as much. The Avaricious man praayed to have a room full of gold. No sooner said than done; but all his joy was turned to grieff when he found that his neighbor had two rooms full of the precious metall. Then came the turn of the Envious man, whoo could not bear to think that his neighbor had any joy at all. So he asked the king that he might have one of his own eyes covered, by which means his neighbor would have both of his covvered.

Vices are their own punishment.

Avaricious and Envious (correct version)

Two neighbors came before the king and asked him **to** grant their hearts' desire. Now the one was full of **avarice**, and the other eaten up with **envy**. **So** to punish them both, the king granted that each might have **whatever** he wished for himself, but only **on** the condition that his neighbor had twice as much. The Avaricious man **prayed** to have a room full of gold. No sooner said than done; but all his joy was turned to **grief** when he found that his neighbor had two rooms full of the precious **metal**. Then came the turn of the Envious man, **who** could not bear to think that his neighbor had any joy at all. So he asked the king that he might have one of his own eyes covered, by which means his neighbor would have both of his **covered**.

Vices are their own punishment.

The following passage contains homophones that are incorrect. Can you find them?

The Boasting Traveler

A man who had crossed the see and traveled in for-end lands boasted very much; after returning to his own country, of the mini wonderful and heroic feets he had performed in the different places he had visited. He loved to tell his tails. Among other things, he said that when he was at Roads he had leaped to such a distance that no man of his day could leap anywhere near him as to that, there were in Rhodes many persons who saw him do it and whom he could call as witnesses. Won of the bystanders interrupted him, saying: "Now, my dear man, if this tail be all true there is no need of witnesses. Suppose this to be Roads, and leap four us."

He who does a thing well does not need to boast

The Boasting Traveler (correct version)

A man who had crossed the **sea** and traveled in **foreign** lands boasted very much; after returning to his own country, of the **many** wonderful and heroic **feats** he had performed in the different places he had visited. He loved to tell his **tales**. Among other things, he said that when he was at **Rhodes** he had leaped to such a distance that no man of his day could leap anywhere near him as to that, there were in Rhodes many persons who saw him do it and whom he could call as witnesses. **One** of the bystanders interrupted him, saying: "Now, my dear man, if this **tale** be all true there is no need of witnesses. Suppose this to be **Rhodes**, and leap **for** us."

He who does a thing well does not need to boast.

The next passage contains more homophones that are incorrect. Can you find them?

The Wind and the Son

The Wind and the Son were disputing witch was the stronger. They saw a traveler coming down the rode, and the Son said: "I sea a way too decide are dispute. Witchever of us can cause that traveller too take off his cloak shall bee regarded as the stronger. Ewe begin."

The Son retired behind a cloud, and the Wind began too blow as hard as it could upon the traveller. But the harder he blue the more closely did the traveller rap his cloak round him, till at last the Wind had too give up in despair. Then the Son came out and shone in all his glory upon the traveller, who soon found it to hot too walk with his cloak on.

Kindness effects more than severity.

The Wind and the Sun (correct version)

The Wind and the **Sun** were disputing **which** was the stronger. They saw a traveler coming down the **road**, and the **Sun** said: "I **see** a way **to** decide **our** dispute. **Whichever** of us can cause that traveller **to** take off his cloak shall **be** regarded as the stronger. **You** begin."

The **Sun** retired behind a cloud, and the Wind began **to** blow as hard as it could upon the traveller. But the harder he **blew** the more closely did the traveller **wrap** his cloak round him, till at last the Wind had **to** give up in despair. Then the Sun came out and shone in all his glory upon the traveller, who soon found it **too** hot **to** walk with his cloak on.

Kindness effects more than severity.

This next passage contains coma-splices. Can you find them?

The Crow and the Raven

The Crow was jealous of the Raven because he was considered a bird of good omen. Raven always attracted the attention of men, they noted by his flight the good or bad course of future events. Seeing some travelers approaching, the Crow flew up into a tree, perching herself on one of the branches, she cawed as loudly as she could. The travelers turned toward the sound and wondered what it foreboded, one of them then said to his companion, "Let us proceed on our journey, my friend, for it is only the caw of a crow, and her cry, you know, is no omen."

Those who assume a character that does not belong to them, only make themselves ridiculous.

The Crow and the Raven (correct version)

The crow was jealous of the Raven because he was considered a bird of good omen. Raven always attracted the attention of men; they noted by his flight the good or bad course of future events. Seeing some travelers approaching, the Crow flew up into a tree; perching herself on one of the branches, she cawed as loudly as she could. The travelers turned toward the sound and wondered what it foreboded; one of them then said to his companion, "Let us proceed on our journey, my friend, for it is only the caw of a crow, and her cry, you know, is no omen."

Those who assume a character that does not belong to them, only make themselves ridiculous.

This passage also contains coma-splices. Can you find them?

The Goose with the Golden Eggs

One day a countryman looked into the nest of his Goose, there he found an egg, all yellow and glittering. He picked it up, it was as heavy as lead. He was going to throw it away because he thought a trick had been played upon him. He took it home, soon he found, to his delight, that it was an egg of pure gold. Every morning, the same thing occurred, and he soon became rich by selling his eggs. As he grew rich, he grew greedy, and thinking to get at once all the gold the Goose could give, he killed it and opened it. He looked inside, he found nothing.

Greed oft o'er reaches itself.

The Goose with the Golden Eggs (correct version)

One day a countryman looked into the nest of his Goose; there he found an egg, all yellow and glittering. He picked it up; it was as heavy as lead. He was going to throw it away because he thought a trick had been played upon him. He took it home; soon he found, to his delight, that it was an egg of pure gold. Every morning, the same thing occurred, and he soon became rich by selling his eggs. As he grew rich, he grew greedy; and thinking to get at once all the gold the Goose could give, he killed it and opened it. He looked inside; he found nothing.

Greed oft o'er reaches itself.

The following passage contains sentence fragments (some words are missing). Can you find and correct them?

The Fir-Tree and the Thornbush

A Fir-Tree to the Thornbush, "You are useful for nothing at all. No one likes you. You full of thorns. Not tall and beautiful like I am. Besides, no one uses you for anything. My wood, however, is used to make houses and schools. Fences and frames. Axe and hammer handles." The Thornbush, "You poor creature, do you really think you're so much better? More desirable than me? How many of you are hacked down every year? With those very same axes you become handles for? If you think about it, you might have reason to wish that you had grown up. A Thornbush, not a Fir-Tree."

Better poverty without care, than riches with.

The Fir-Tree and the Thornbush (correct version)

A Fir-Tree boasted to the Thornbush, "You are useful for nothing at all. No one likes you. You are full of thorns. You are not tall and beautiful like I am. Besides, no one uses you for anything. My wood, however, is used to make houses and schools, fences and frames, axe and hammer handles." The Thornbush answered, "You poor creature, do you really think you're so much better and more desirable than me? How many of you are hacked down every year with those very same axes you become handles for? If you think about it, you might have reason to wish that you had grown up a Thornbush, not a Fir-Tree."

Better poverty without care, than riches with.

The following passage contains more sentence fragments (some words are missing from the passage). Can you find and correct them?

The Fox and the Goat

A Fox fell into a deep well and could find no means of escape. A thirsty Goat to the same well. Seeing the Fox. The Goat asked if the water was. Pretending to be happy. The Fox praised the water; he told the Goat that it was the sweetest water he had ever tasted. He then encouraged the Goat to jump into the well so that he could taste the water and quench his thirst. The Goat, mindful only of his dry mouth. Thoughtlessly jumped into the well. As the Goat drank, the Fox told him. That they were both now trapped in the bottom of the well. The Fox, however, had a scheme for their escape. "If you will place your forefeet upon the wall and bend your head," said the Fox, "I will run up your back and escape. I will you out afterward." The Goat did as he said, and the Fox leaped his back. Steadying himself with the Goat's horns. The Fox safely reached the mouth of the well. And said goodbye to the Goat. When the Goat yelled at him for breaking his promise, the Fox turned and said, "You foolish fellow! If you had as many brains in your head as you have hairs in your beard, you would never have jumped into the well without having thought of a way out first."

Look before you leap.

The Fox and the Goat (correct version)

A Fox fell into a deep well and could find no means of escape. A thirsty Goat came to the same well. Seeing the Fox, the Goat asked if the water was good. Pretending to be happy, the Fox praised the water; he told the Goat that it was the sweetest water he had ever tasted. He then encouraged the Goat to jump into the well so that he could taste the water and quench his thirst. The Goat, mindful only of his dry mouth, thoughtlessly jumped into the well. As the Goat drank, the Fox told him that they were both now trapped in the bottom of the well. The Fox, however, had a scheme for their escape. "If you will place your forefeet upon the wall and bend your head," said the Fox, "I will run up your back and escape. I will help you out afterward." The Goat did as he said, and the Fox leaped upon his back. Steadying himself with the Goat's horns, the Fox safely reached the mouth of the well and said goodbye to the Goat. When the Goat yelled at him for breaking his promise, the Fox turned and said, "You foolish fellow! If you had as many brains in your head as you have hairs in your beard, you would never have jumped into the well without having thought of a way out first."

Look before you leap.

Add periods in the correct places in the following passages. Be sure to capitalize the word that begins each sentence.

The Wolf in Sheep's Clothing

a Wolf found great difficulty in getting at the sheep owing to the vigilance of the shepherd and his dogs one day it found the skin of a sheep that had been flayed and thrown aside the Wolf put the sheepskin on over its own pelt and strolled down among the sheep the Lamb that belonged to the sheep, whose skin the Wolf was wearing, began to follow the Wolf in the Sheep's clothing leading the Lamb a little apart, the Wolf soon made a meal of her for the next few days, the Wolf succeeded in deceiving the sheep and enjoying hearty meals.

appearances are deceptive

The Wolf in Sheep's Clothing (correct version)

A Wolf found great difficulty in getting at the sheep owing to the vigilance of the shepherd and his dogs. One day it found the skin of a sheep that had been flayed and thrown aside. The Wolf put the sheepskin on over its own pelt and strolled down among the sheep. The Lamb that belonged to the sheep, whose skin the Wolf was wearing, began to follow the Wolf in the Sheep's clothing. Leading the Lamb a little apart, the Wolf soon made a meal of her. For the next few days, the Wolf succeeded in deceiving the sheep and enjoying hearty meals.

Appearances are deceptive.

Add periods in the correct places in the following passage. Be sure to capitalize the word that begins each sentence.

The Miser

a miser sold all that he had and bought a lump of gold, which he buried in a hole in the ground by the side of an old wall he went to look at it daily one of his workmen observed the miser's frequent visits to the spot and decided to watch his movements the workman soon discovered the secret of the hidden treasure and, digging down, came to the lump of gold, and stole it

the miser, on his next visit, found the hole empty and began to tear his hair and to make loud lamentations a neighbor, seeing him overcome with grief and learning the cause, said, "pray do not grieve so; go and take a stone, and place it in the hole, and fancy that the gold is still lying there it will do you quite the same service; for when the gold was there, you had it not, as you did not make the slightest use of it"

The Miser (correct version)

A miser sold all that he had and bought a lump of gold, which he buried in a hole in the ground by the side of an old wall. He went to look at it daily. One of his workmen observed the miser's frequent visits to the spot and decided to watch his movements. The workman soon discovered the secret of the hidden treasure and, digging down, came to the lump of gold, and stole it.

The miser, on his next visit, found the hole empty and began to tear his hair and to make loud lamentations. A neighbor, seeing him overcome with grief and learning the cause, said, "Pray do not grieve so; go and take a stone, and place it in the hole, and fancy that the gold is still lying there. It will do you quite the same service; for when the gold was there, you had it not, as you did not make the slightest use of it."

The verbs in this passage are incorrect; can you correct them?

The Two Fellows and the Bear

Two Fellows was travelling together through a wood, when a Bear rush out upon them. One of the travelers happening to be in front, and he seize hold of the branch of a tree, and hidded himself among the leaves. The other, sawing no help for it, throwed himself flat down upon the ground, with his face in the dust. The Bear, walk up to him, putted his muzzle close to his ear, and sniff and sniff. But at last, with a growl, he shaked his head and slouch off, for bears do not touching dead meat. Then the fellow in the tree jump down to his comrade, and, laughing, say, "What is it that Master Bruin will whisper to you?"

"He telled me," say the other, "Never trusted a friend who desert you at a pinch."

The Two Fellows and the Bear (correct version)

Two Fellows **were travelling** together through a wood, when a Bear **rushed** out upon them. One of the travelers **happened to be** in front, and he **seized** hold of the branch of a tree, and **hid** himself among the leaves. The other, **seeing** no help for it, **threw** himself flat down upon the ground, with his face in the dust. The Bear, **coming** up to him, **put** his muzzle close to his ear, and **sniffed** and **sniffed**. But at last, with a growl, he **shook** his head and **slouched** off, for bears **will not touch** dead meat. Then the fellow in the tree **jumped** down to his comrade, and, laughing, **said**, "What **was** it that Master Bruin **whispered** to you?"

"He **told** me," **said** the other, "Never **trust** a friend who **deserts** you at a pinch."

The verbs in this passage are incorrect; can you correct them?

The Hare and the Tortoise

A Hare one day maded fun of the short feet and slow pace of the Tortoise. The Tortoise say in reply, "Though you is swift as the wind, I could of beat you in a race." The Hare, believe that the Tortoise was crazy, agree to the race; they both agreeing that the Fox should chose the course and been the judge. On the day appointed for the race the two starting together. The Tortoise never for a moment stop, but goed on with a slow but steady pace straight to the end of the course. The Hare, lie down by the wayside, falled fast asleep. At last waking up, and moving as fast as he could, he seen the Tortoise had done reached the goal, and was comfortably dozed after her fatigue.

Slow but steady wins the race.

The Hare and the Tortoise (correct version)

A Hare one day **made** fun of the short feet and slow pace of the Tortoise. The Tortoise **said** in reply, "Though you **are** swift as the wind, I **can beat** you in a race." The Hare, **believing** that the Tortoise was crazy, **agreed** to the race; they both **agreed** that the Fox should **choose** the course and **be** the judge. On the day appointed for the race the two **started** together. The Tortoise never for a moment **stopped**, but **went** on with a slow but steady pace straight to the end of the course. The Hare, **lying** down by the wayside, **fell** fast asleep. At last waking up, and moving as fast as he could, he **saw** the Tortoise **had reached** the goal, and was comfortably **dozing** after her fatigue.

Slow but steady wins the race.

This passage has no punctuation and no capital letters. Add the appropriate punctuation and capital letters.

the frog and the ox

oh father said a little frog to the big one sitting by the side of a pool ive seen a terrible monster it was as big as a mountain it had horns as big as trees a tail like a snake and hooves divided in two

tush child tush said the old frog that was only farmer whites ox it ist so big either he may be a little bit taller than i, but i could easily make myself quite as broad just you see so he blew himself out and blew himself out and blew himself out

was he as big as that he asked

oh, much bigger than that said the young frog

again the old one blew himself out and asked the young one if the ox was as big as that

bigger father bigger was the reply

so the frog took a deep breath and blew and blew and blew and swelled and swelled and swelled and then he said im sure the farmers ox is not as big as this

at that moment however he burst

self conceit may lead to self destruction

The Frog and the Ox (correct version)

"Oh, Father," said a little Frog to the big one sitting by the side of a pool, "I've seen a terrible monster! It was as big as a mountain; it had horns as big as trees, a tail like a snake, and hooves divided in two."

"Tush, child, tush," said the old Frog, "that was only Farmer White's ox. It isn't so big either; he may be a little bit taller than I, but I could easily make myself quite as broad; just you see." So he blew himself out, and blew himself out, and blew himself out.

"Was he as big as that?" he asked.

"Oh, much bigger than that," said the young frog.

Again the old one blew himself out, and asked the young one if the ox was as big as that.

"Bigger, Father, bigger," was the reply.

So the frog took a deep breath, and blew and blew and blew, and swelled and swelled and swelled. And then he said, "I'm sure the farmer's ox is not as big as this."

At that moment, however, he burst.

Self-conceit may lead to self-destruction.

This passage has no punctuation and no capital letters. Add the appropriate punctuation and capital letters.

the fox who lost his tail

an old shaggy grey fox got caught in a trap even though he managed to escape he lost his tail in the process for days after his escape feeling his life a burden from the shame and ridicule of being the only tailless fox in the county he schemed to convince all the other foxes to cut off their tails he assembled a good many foxes and advised them to cut off their tails saying that they would not only look much better without them but that they would get rid of the weight of the brush which was a very great inconvenience one of them interrupted him and said just because you were dumb enough to lose your tail don't ask us to do the same

The Fox Who Lost His Tail (correct version)

An old, shaggy, grey fox got caught in a trap. Even though he managed to escape, he lost his tail in the process. For days after his escape, feeling his life a burden from the shame and ridicule of being the only tailless fox in the county, he schemed to convince all the other foxes to cut off their tails. He assembled a good many foxes and advised them to cut off their tails, saying that they would not only look much better without them, but that they would get rid of the weight of the brush, which was a very great inconvenience. One of them interrupted him and said, "Just because you were dumb enough to lose your tail, don't ask us to do the same."

The following sentences are out of order; can you put them in their proper sequence?

The Fox and the Crow

1. The Crow settled on a branch of a tree.
2. "I'm sure your voice must surpass that of other birds, just as your figure does."
3. Casually, he walked up to the foot of the tree.
4. "I'll find a way to get that cheese for myself," said the Fox to himself.
5. "Good-day, Mistress Crow," he cried.
6. "That was all I wanted," he added, "and in exchange for your cheese I will give you a piece of advice for the future: do not trust flatterers."
7. It was snapped up by the Fox.
8. A Fox once saw a Crow fly off with a piece of cheese in its beak.
9. "How lovely you look today: how glossy your feathers, how bright your eye.
10. The Crow lifted up her head and began to caw her best, but the moment she opened her mouth the piece of cheese fell to the ground.
11. "That will do," he said.
12. "Let me hear but one song from you that I may tell all of my friends that you are the Queen of Birds."

The Fox and the Crow (correct version)

A Fox once saw a Crow fly off with a piece of cheese in its beak. The Crow settled on a branch of a tree. "I'll find a way to get that cheese for myself," said the Fox to himself. Casually, he walked up to the foot of the tree. "Good-day, Mistress Crow," he cried.

"How lovely you look today: how glossy your feathers, how bright your eye. I'm sure your voice must surpass that of other birds, just as your figure does. Let me hear but one song from you that I may tell all of my friends that you are the Queen of Birds." The Crow lifted up her head and began to caw her best, but the moment she opened her mouth the piece of cheese fell to the ground. It was snapped up the Fox. "That will do," he said. "That was all I wanted," he added, "and in exchange for your cheese I will give you a piece of advice for the future: do not trust flatterers."

The following sentences are out of order; can you put them in their proper sequence?

The Fox and the Grapes

1. He ran and jumped again, but with no greater success.
2. "Just the thing to quench my thirst," said the Fox.
3. One hot summer day a Fox was strolling through an orchard.
4. Again and again he tried after the tempting morsel.
5. Walking away with his nose in the air, he said to himself, "I am sure those grapes are sour."
6. He backed up a few feet.
7. It is easy to despise what you cannot get.
8. Panting and weary, he finally gave up.
9. Looking up, he spied a bunch of Grapes just ripening on a vine that was hanging over a lofty branch.
10. Each time, however, he missed the grapes.
11. Then, he took a run and a jump, but he just missed the grapes.

The Fox and the Grapes (correct version)

One hot summer day a Fox was strolling through an orchard. Looking up, he spied a bunch of Grapes just ripening on a vine that was hanging over a lofty branch. "Just the thing to quench my thirst," said the Fox. He backed up a few feet. Then, he took a run and a jump, but he just missed the grapes. He ran and jumped again, but with no greater success. Again and again he tried after the tempting morsel. Each time, however, he missed the grapes. Panting and weary, he finally gave up. Walking away with his nose in the air, he said to himself, "I am sure those grapes are sour."

It is easy to despise what you cannot get.

Poetry Patterns

One of the easiest, most rewarding, and most successful ways to entice young writers into the world of formally arranged words is to introduce them to poetic patterns. Poetic patterns are, after grammatical elements and word play, the necessary third step in the process of enabling young writers to achieve immediate, discernible success in writing.

The purpose of this process is for students to plunge directly into texts so that they can discover meaning in immediate and dynamic ways. And because the outcome of their meaning-making forays will be pattern poems, students must simply follow the directions given for each. Rather than having to wrestle with the many interlocking aspects of writing that often befuddle beginning writers—the procedures for producing a form and its variations—young writers are free to follow simple directions as they work to construct poems that are short and clear. Accordingly, when students write pattern poems, they will no longer ask, "How long does my poem have to be?" or "How do I write this?" Rather, they will understand the requirements of the poem from the directions; they will consciously construct the poem, as opposed to simply letting words pour out of them without restraint or thought.

Additionally, as writers construct pattern poems, they will discover how the precise use of writer's tools—the sixteen elements of grammar that they've already learned—can enable them to generate and convey thoughts, ideas, and images that they would not have been otherwise able to do.

Build-a-Name Poetry

Cinderella has many counterparts in other lands. The Norwegian Cinderella is called *Cinderlad* in the story "The Princess on the Glass Hill." In the Italian variation, *Cenerentola* throws coins as she leaves the ball. The Micmac Indian names her *Little Burnt Face*. *Ash Maiden* is the German Cinderella, who is granted her wish by a white dove. The English *Tattercoats* receives her lovely ball gown from the herdboy.

Use the letters of the name of one of the Cinderellas from another country to begin each line of a poem.

EXAMPLE:

T welve o'clock
A nd
T ime to escape
T he changing that will
E nd her dream
R unning, faster and faster,
C inderella escapes
O nly to return
A gain
T o
S itting alone by the fire.

Using variations of Cinderella or other fairy-tale characters, write a poem telling about the experiences the character has.

Diamante

A *diamante* is a poem written in the shape of a diamond. It progresses from a short line through lines of increasing length and returns again to a short line. The diamante also uses specific parts of speech.

Use the following pattern:

In line one give the name of the character.

In line two use an adjective-noun combination to describe the character (the noun in this line should be a synonym for the character).

In line three give three present participles that describe something about the character.

In line four give either four past participles or a combination of past participles and adjectives that further describe the character.

In line five give another synonym for the character.

And, for an added twist, try using alliteration.

noun

adjective noun

three describing words (*-ing* words: present participles)

four describing words (*-ed* words: past participles, if possible)

noun

EXAMPLES:

Rapunzel

morose maiden

looking longing languishing

disgusted disgruntled dejected demoted

daughter

Wolf (Big Bad)

corybantic canine

bullying blustering bellowing

determined destructive devious dangerous

carnivore

Wishing upon a Poem

Wishing need not be only on stars. Wishing can be in poems. We have all wished we were something else, real or make-believe. This is a form of cinquain (a five-line stanza) used to tell what the poet wishes.

Use this pattern:

Line 1: "I wish I were"
Line 2: Who would you like to be
Line 3: Where would you like to be (prepositional phrase)
Line 4: What would you like to be doing, usually an *-ing* word (gerund or participle, depending on usage)
Line 5: How would you be doing it

EXAMPLES:

Cinderella
I wish I were
A princess
At a royal ball
Dancing a waltz
Gliding and spinning perfectly.

Ogre
I wish I were
an opera singer
on opening night
singing on the stage
each note pitched perfectly

Big Bad Wolf
I wish I were
A race car driver
at the Indy 500
Revving my engine, peeling out, winning first place
Adroitly in my car named the *pork-mobile*.

Now try your own.

Bio-Poem

A bio-poem is a short biography telling about the life of someone, either real or literary. Select a favorite fairy-tale character and write a bio-poem using the following pattern.

Line 1 First name only _____

Line 2 Four traits (adj) _____

Line 3 Related to _____

Line 4 Cares deeply about _____

Line 5 Who feels _____

Line 6 Who needs _____

Line 7 Who gives _____

Line 8 Who fears _____

Line 9 Who'd like to see _____

Line 10 Resident of _____

Here's an example:

Gretel
Small, lost, tired, hungry,
Sister of Hansel,
Cares deeply about her caged brother,
Who feels confused and confined,
Who needs a place to escape to,
Who gives companionship,
Who fears the witch,
Who would like to see her father again,
Resident of the forest.

Night Poem

Night can be a very strange time. Think of all the things that might happen "One Minute after Midnight."

Try writing a five-stanza poem. In each stanza tell what happens one minute after midnight. Here are two stanzas to start you off:

One minute after midnight
    black is the dominant color.
One minute after midnight
    spiders spin webs of dreams.
One minute after midnight
    owls hoot and haunt thick forests.
One minute after midnight
    stars begin to people-gaze.
One minute after midnight
    Words dance in books while authors sleep.

One minute after midnight
    Ogres prowl the night-shrouded countryside
One minute after midnight
    Enchanted frogs croak at the luminous moon
One minute after midnight
    Dragons rouse themselves from slumber
One minute after midnight
    Trees talk to one another in a leafy language
One minute after midnight
    Beanstalks grow in the dreams of sleepers

Now write your own five-stanza poem.

Alliterative Poem

An *alliterative poem* provides an excellent method to describe characters, people, animals, objects, places, and events. Here are some examples:

The Frog Prince

For breakfast he loved to munch on
    flirtatious
    flamboyant
    flabby
    flies.

At noon he loved to lunch on
    gnarled
    gnashing
    gnawing
    gnats.

For dinner he loved to crunch on
    speaking
    spunky
    spectacular
    spiders.

The Giant

For breakfast he loved to munch on
    plump
    perfect
    prodigious
    pancakes.

At noon he loved to lunch on
    huge
    heavy
    hefty
    hero sandwiches.

For dinner he loved to crunch on
    massive
    mammoth
    mountainous
    mashed potatoes.

Now try your own.

Alliterative Character Poem

The use of alliteration is a key to writing about character. Useful tools are a dictionary and thesaurus. Use the pattern to write about a favorite character.

Line One: Name the character.

Line Two: Use at least four words beginning with the first letter of the character's name to tell where it lives.

Line Three: Use at least four words beginning with the same letter to tell what the character eats or does.

Line Four: Using the same letter, tell four things the character likes to do.

Line Five: The last line (using as many words with the same letter as possible) tell about some special power or talent the character has.

EXAMPLE:

Rapunzel

Resides reluctantly in a rough round room.

Rapunzel relishes rotund ripe raspberries.

Rapunzel rolls and unrolls her rich radiant hair.

Rapunzel unwraps her hair to the royal prince riding a regal steed.

Parts of Speech Poem

This poem enables you to use your knowledge of the seven parts of speech to describe a character. To be successful, you must use specific parts of speech.

Use this pattern:

1 article (a, an, the)—1 noun (name of a character)
    1 adjective—1 conjunction—1 adjective
1 verb—1 conjunction—1 verb
    1 adverb
        1 noun that relates to the noun in the first line

Here are two examples:

The Stonecutter
    Poor but imaginative
Cleaves and calls
    Desperately—
        Fool

The (third) Pig
    calm and clever
plans and prepares
    craftily
        builder

Now try your own.

Adverb Poem

Adverbs are often overlooked by many writers when they first put pen to paper. Here's a pattern poem that invites you to use adverbs (plus other parts of speech) to write about a favorite character.

Use this pattern:

Adverb
adverb
adverb
article—noun
verb
noun + prepositional phrase

EXAMPLES:

The Weaver ("Rumplestiltskin")
Humbly,
wretchedly,
desperately,
the weaver
pleads
to the greedy king.

Snow White
Silently,
serenely,
somnolently,
the maiden
sleeps
for years and years.

Another Parts of Speech Poem

Choose a character or an object from a story. Use the following pattern to write about it.

Noun
Verb, verb, verb
Prepositional phrase (where the verb happens)
Prepositional phrase (where the verb happens)
Prepositional phrase (where the verb happens)
Noun (restates, or is a synonym for, the noun in the first line)

EXAMPLES:

Troll
Seethes, bristles, rages,
Beneath the bridge,
    From dusk
    'Till dawn—
Tyrant!

Goldilocks
Eats, breaks, sleeps
In the house
    Up the stairs
    In the bed—
House-wrecker!

Giant
Stomps, tromps, bellows
In the house
    Across the clouds,
    Down the stalk—
Behemoth!

Prepositional Phrase Poem

Choose a favorite character or object. Use the following pattern to write about it. Try to use as much alliteration as you can.

Prepositional phrase (location)
   Prepositional phrase (location)
      Prepositional phrase (location)
         Prepositional phrase (location)
            Verb + adjective + adjective
            Noun

EXAMPLES:

Near the twisted path,
   Beyond the burnt oak tree,
      In the dark, dingy cave,
         Beside the cold stalactites
            Sleeps a sulphuric smokey
          Dragon.

Above the quiet village,
   Atop the craggy mountain,
      Between withering trees,
         On the floor of a dry riverbed
            Sits a rough-skinned magic
          Toad.

Past the stone bridge,
   In a distant land,
      Inside the castle,
         On the shiny dance floor
            Twirls a smiling, beaming
          Cinderella.

Participial Phrase Poem

Choose a favorite character or object. Use the following pattern to write about it.

Participial phrase
Participial phrase
Participial phrase
Adjective + Noun
Verb + direct object
Prepositional phrase (where)

EXAMPLES:

Sitting on a lily pad,
Gazing at the moon,
Waiting for a princess,
The enchanted frog
Gobbled flies
On the edge of the pond.

Sobbing bitterly,
Wringing her hands,
Wiping tears from her one eye,
The strange stepsister
Watched Cinderella's wedding
In the royal hall.

Holding his breath,
Hiding behind the huge chair,
Hoping he wouldn't be caught,
A trembling Jack
Heard the giant roar
On the front steps.

Sentence Pattern Poems

Write about a favorite character by using the following pattern:

Adjective + Noun
Verb + direct object
Prepositional phrase (where)
Prepositional phrase (when)

EXAMPLES:

The dejected wolf
Opened a TV dinner
In his dim den
At midnight.

The seven dwarfs
Formed their own little rap group
In Oz's corporate headquarters
On the first day of the month.

A nervous Odysseus
Opened the trapdoor of the wooden horse
Outside the gates of Troy
At dawn.

Now write about a favorite character by using this pattern:

Adjective + noun
Verb + direct object
Prepositional phrase (where)
Adjective clause (why)

EXAMPLES:

The dejected wolf
Opened a TV dinner
In his dim den
Because he had failed to bring home any pork.

The seven dwarfs
Formed their own little rap group
In Oz's corporate headquarters
Because they were tired of whistling while they worked.

A nervous Odysseus
Opened the trapdoor of the wooden horse
Outside the gates of Troy
Because the Trojans had all fallen asleep.

Syllable Poems

In these poems, each line has a specific number of syllables. The idea is to choose words that are precise in both syllabic count and in their ability to communicate ideas.

Use the following pattern:

Four syllables
Four syllables
Five syllables
Five syllables
Seven syllables
Seven syllables

EXAMPLES:

Jack

How poor I am!
How rich I'll be
If I climb this stalk
To the land above.
Golden eggs and golden coins
Are the gleaming things I seek.

Giant

Hungry I am!
And full I'll be
When I seize and bake
That bold, sneaky boy
Who's got stealing on his mind.
Oh, what a fine snack he'll be!

This poem is a variation. Try this pattern:

One syllable
Two syllables
Three syllables
Four syllables
Five syllables

EXAMPLES:

Bats!

Dark flock—
Together
In the night sky.
Twist, flutter, and fly!

Troll

Fuming
Wrathfully—
Wishing that goats
Had never been born.

Frog

Green prince
with two
webbed back feet
He longs for lips
And a magic kiss.

Syllable Question Poem

This syllable poem is different from the others because it takes the form of a question.

Here's the pattern:

Seven syllables
Five syllables
Three syllables

EXAMPLES:

Goats plan to cross the stone bridge.
Do they see the sole
Troll beneath?

Red Riding Hood met the wolf
In grandmother's bed.
Where's Red now?

At midnight Cinderella
Lost her glass slipper.
Who has it?

Rapunzel let down her hair.
Did she know she'd snag
A husband?

Text Message Poem

Write a poem in the form of a "text message" from one folktale character to another. Use as few letters as possible; use numbers in place of words. The message should be concrete and contain figurative language.

EXAMPLES:

from: red riding hood
to: 3 pigs

just met a wolf 2day—
lots o teeth, 2 many 2 count—
hope ur build'n strong houses—
b alert! u never know when he
might head ur way

from: 3 pigs
to: red riding hood

thanks 4 ur text—
w/ ur warning we r ready
4 the wolf—
who's afraid of the
b b wolf?

from: wolf
to: 3 pigs

saw ur 1st 2 houses—
is that the best u can do?
just 8 but still hungry—
lungs ready 4 work!
c u 2morrow—

Acts of Writing: Putting It All Together with Process Writing

The activities in this section of the book, which focus on some of the forms that children need to learn to use to become stronger writers, are designed to be starting points. As such, they guide children in the creation of clearly defined texts.

Each activity moves through the writing process: prewriting, drafting, revising, editing/sharing. In the prewriting stage, don't worry about what you're going to write or how you're going to write it, just spend time coming up with lots of ideas. The more ideas you come up with, the more choices you will have when you begin to write. In the drafting stage, take ideas you came up with in prewriting and use them in the writing form that you are crafting. In the revising stage, try to get rid of weak or abstract nouns, verbs, adjectives, and adverbs. Replace them with ones that are more vivid and specific. Also, where you can, add phrases and clauses. These will make your writing more solid. In the editing stage, look for misspelled words, punctuation errors, or grammatical errors. In the sharing stage, either read your writing aloud or put it in a class book.

These activities slow down the teaching of writing so that children can take their time to successfully and thoughtfully move through each step of the writing process. It is important, though, to recognize that the prewriting stage is the most important step of the writing process, and that writers should spend something like 70 percent of their time at this stage. This point cannot be stressed too much.

It is also a good idea for the teacher to join the children when they write and to create her own examples of the activities in this chapter. In this way, the teacher can come to an experiential understanding of what the children are doing, what problems they might encounter, and ways to help them solve those problems.

The easiest way to use these activities is to follow the directions in the order they are given. During the prewriting stage of each activity the teacher should have a conversation with the children—especially when brainstorming—and write the children's prewriting ideas and brainstorming lists on a blackboard or transparency on an overhead projector. Such written lists will serve as reference points and will stimulate ideas as the children begin to draft.

The drafting stage of each activity allows the teacher to model for children the various forms they are writing and also to teach minilessons on various grammatical structures that children can use (some are already built into the lessons).

During the revising and editing stage of each activity, the teacher should invite the children to work in groups and to use the directions for these stages as rubrics against which students can check their own work and the work of their partners. As the children move into these stages, they will consciously choose and use combinations of the sixteen essential elements of grammar.

Once children have prewritten, drafted, revised, and edited, have them share their work with one another, either in small or in large groups. Sharing is the key to creating a community of readers and writers. And children will share their writings most effectively if they do not read their writings "cold," but practice by using the skills of vocal variety. As children share their writings aloud, they will become part of a lively, oral community of readers and writers. By becoming part of such a community, children will have a stronger investment in wanting to create interesting texts because they know they will be sharing them with their peers. Also, children will be more interested in effectively reading what they have written because they know they will have a live and engaged audience. When children become part of such a community, they find authentic reasons to read, write, and share.

The activities can be modified for children with different developmental or writing abilities. For young children, the writing guide can simplify the activities by reducing the sentence length, the structure of the forms, or the kinds of figurative language the children might use.

Five Recursive Steps in the Writing Process

1. PREWRITING: Seventy percent of a writer's time should be spent generating ideas for writing. At this stage, writers should consider: subject, audience, purpose, form, and specific ways to generate and organize ideas. Prewriting strategies include (but are not limited to): reading aloud, brainstorming, clustering, freewriting, conversing, questioning, daydreaming, imaging, wondering, arguing, webbing, rewriting other works, sharing words, telling jokes, finding rhymes, looking at homophones, creating similes and metaphors, and playing with language patterns.

2. DRAFTING: After rehearsing ideas, writers should choose the best forms for their writing and begin constructing them; they should take their best ideas from the prewriting stage and move them into the forms they have chosen. At this stage, writers should not edit; that is, they should not be overly concerned with mechanical matters.

3. REVISING: Writers look at their work (and ask someone else to) and try to reimagine it; that is, to see it from a new point of view in order to find new ideas or betters ways of expressing the ideas in the writing. (Writers might use more rehearsing strategies at this point.) At this stage, minilessons can be introduced: grammar and usage items, patterns and structures.

4. EDITING: (attending to syntactic, stylistic, and/or mechanical matters): Writers "clean up" their writing by making sure that it is free from syntactic, grammatical, usage, spelling, and punctuation errors. This is often a tedious and difficult stage, but it is absolutely essential.

5. SHARING/PUBLISHING: Once the work has been edited, it should be read aloud.

Activities and Ideas to Support Poetry Writing

Read poetry out loud to your students, *all* students, every day. As you read, point out what writers do: focus on word choice, deployment of images, rhythm, rhyme, use of figurative language—and how all these work together to achieve a unified effect. As students hear more and more poetry read aloud, they will slowly begin to assimilate the language they hear. As they do, their writing will begin to reflect that kind of language—the language of established poets.

Do an author study. Have the class, either as a whole or in small groups, choose a poet to study. Have the students read many of the poet's poems to decide what topics the poet normally explores and what poetic elements the poet uses. Students make a record of these discoveries in their poetry notebooks, where students also record favorite words, favorite poems, drafts of poems they are writing, and poetic discoveries they make throughout each week.

Designate an area of the room as the poetry area. In this area are books and magazines devoted to poetry. Work to create a rich and diverse collection of poems and poets.

A note to the teacher:

Younger writers may need to create works that are shorter in length, have fewer details, and have fewer phrases and clauses. Feel free to shorten or modify these activities to meet the needs of your students.

Writing Activity I: A "Do You Remember When" Poem

Imagine that you are telling a friend about all the adventures you had together. You can write either about yourself or about a character from something you have read.

Prewriting: Make a list of things you have done. The list can be real or made up.
Example: one ogre talking to another ogre:

> played tricks on the elves
> took the magician's magic hat
> put electric eels in the castle moat
> got caught in the dwarf's tunnel
> scared the troll
> almost got burned by the dragon

Drafting: Choose the best four items from your list; put them in a stanza. Begin with the line, "Do you remember when we . . ." Follow each line with a verb (past tense) phrase:

> Do you remember when we
> played tricks on the elves,
> took the magician's magic hat,
> put electric eels in the castle moat,
> went into the dragon's cave?

Revising: Add more information to each of the four lines. Use strong nouns and verbs; add or get rid of words. Add phrases and clauses.

> Do you remember when we
> > tricked the elves into thinking
> > we were Elvis come back to rock
> > from the Great Beyond?
>
> Do you remember when we
> > swiped the magician's magic hat,
> > said the wrong spell, and
> > turned ourselves into wrangling rabbits?
>
> Do you remember when we
> > dumped a bucket of baby electric eels
> > into the castle moat
> > the day the royal family went swimming?
>
> Do you remember when we
> > crept into the cold cave
> > to cart off some coins and
> > almost got barbecued by the dragon?

■ How is the revision different from the draft?
What words have been changed?
What phrases have been added?
What clauses have been added?

■ Words that have been changed: swiped (not took), dumped (not put), crept (not went).

■ Prepositional phrases that have been added: from the Great Beyond, into wrangling rabbits, of baby electric eels, into the moat, into the cave, by the dragon.

■ Infinitive phrases that have been added: to rock, to cart off

■ Compound predicate phrases that have been added: *swiped* the magician's magic hat, *said* the wrong spell, and *turned* ourselves into wrangling rabbits; *crept* into the cold cave, almost *got* barbecued.

Editing/Sharing: Check to see that your revision has commas, periods, apostrophes, and question marks in the right places. Check to see that all the words are spelled correctly. Share the poem by reading it aloud.

Assessment Form

The poem has at least one stanza comprised of questions recalling past adventures.

____ Each question focuses on one activity.

____ Each question contains concrete, specific language.

____ Phrases and clauses are used effectively.

____ The ideas and images in the poem fit together; they make sense together, and they work to support the main idea being expressed in the poem.

____ Mechanical, spelling, and punctuation errors have been avoided.

Writing Activity II: A "So Alone" Poem

Imagine that you are describing how it is to be alone. You can either write about yourself or about a character from something you have read.

Prewriting: Think of times when you were alone. Describe what you noticed (saw, heard, touched, tasted, smelled) and how you felt. You can also write from a character's point of view.

Example: Rapunzel

> a tower room, no way out, a table, a chair, a book, the old woman who visits her once a day, frustration, unhappiness

Drafting: Combine the items from step one in a poem. Describe where you are, what you notice, and how you feel (remember the idea is to tell what it is like to be lonely).

> I'm in a tower room
> there's no way out.
> It's lonely here.
> The only things here are
> a table, a chair,
> a book,
> and the old woman
> who visits me
> every day.

Revising: Add more information to each line. Use strong nouns and verbs; add or get rid of words. Avoid using abstract nouns. Add phrases and clauses.

> I have no more numbers
> for counting the days and nights
> I have languished
> in this tower room, this bolted box surrounded by sky,
> that has neither ladder, nor stairs.
> My only companions are
> the table where I've scratched my initials,
> the chair whose padding is flat
> from so much sitting and waiting,
> the book that I have read
> so much that the ink has faded,
> and the crone below
> who makes me cringe and
> whose cracked voice cackles
> for me to let down my hair
> again.

- How is this revision different from the draft?
  What words have been changed?
  What phrases have been added?
  What clauses have been added?

- Words that have been changed: I have no more numbers for counting the days and nights I have languished in this tower room; this bolted box surrounded by sky, that has neither ladder, nor stairs (not "I'm in this tower room.").

- Prepositional phrases that have been added: in this tower room, in the sky, from so much sitting, for me.

- Appositive phrase that has been added: this bolted box surrounded by sky.

- Infinitive phrase that has been added: to let down my hair.

- Adjective clauses that have been added: that has neither ladder, nor stairs; where I've scratched my initials, whose padding is flat, that I have read, who makes me cringe and whose cracked voice cackles.

- Adverbial clause that has been added: that the ink has faded.

Editing/Sharing: Check to see that your revision has commas, periods, apostrophes, and question marks in the right places. Check to see that all the words are spelled correctly. Share the poem by reading it aloud.

Assessment Form

____ The poem has at least one stanza that describes the experience of being alone.

____ The poem is filled with language that appeals to the senses: sight, sound, touch, smell, taste.

____ The poem contains concrete, specific language.

____ Phrases and clauses are used effectively.

____ The ideas and images in the poem fit together; they make sense together, and they work to support the main idea being expressed in the poem.

____ Mechanical, spelling, and punctuation errors have been avoided.

Writing Activity III: A Persuasive Letter-Poem

Prewriting: Think of a few characters from books or stories you have read. Think of the problems that these characters had to overcome. Choose one character and a problem the character has.

Example: Harry Potter wants to get past the three-headed dog.

- List people the character could write to for help. Be specific. Try and think of at least ten.

Examples: a close friend, another wizard, a dog catcher . . .

- Choose one person. Think of ways your character might persuade this person to come and help solve the problem. Think of five to ten reasons.

Drafting: Choose three reasons and, from the character's point of view, write a persuasive letter to a person who can help solve the problem.

- State the major claim (i.e., the problem and what you want the audience of the letter to do) followed by reasons one, two, and three, which appeal to the self-interest of the letter's recipient. End with a concluding sentence, one that wraps up or restates the idea in the first sentence.

Example: (a letter from Harry Potter to Sideshow Sam, a sideshow performer)

Dear Sideshow Sam,
I need your help.
I need to get past
a three-headed dog.
I thought you could
help me because
you are good with dogs.
I read in the paper that
your two-tailed dog ran away
from your sideshow. If
you help me,
you can have the three-headed dog here.
I know a three-headed dog will attract
more people at your show.
I know you will make more
money with a three-headed dog.
You will become famous too. Please help!
All barked out,
Harry Potter

Revising: Change weak nouns and verbs to stronger ones. Add powerful phrases and clauses.

Dear Sideshow Sam,
I read in Bark 'n' Bite magazine
that your two-tailed dog escaped
from your sideshow. I'm sorry for your
bad dog luck, but I may
be able to help. How would you
like a three-headed dog? I know where you
can get your mitts on one!

Such a beast is barring me from exploring
the belly of Hogwarts School.
If you capture the beast,
you'll be barkin' happy!
First, if you had a three-headed dog,
you'd have the most popular
attraction at your carnival. People would be
frothing at the mouth just to get a gander
at the creature. Second, imagine the
money you'd be able to make!
After only three years of displaying the
three-headed beast, you'd be able to make
enough money to retire and live a yap-happy life.
Finally, you'd be able to write a book about

your experiences, travel the talkshow circuit,
be an Oprah book-of-the-month selection,
and maybe even have a TV movie made about you.
Fame would be a bone you could chew on for years and years!

What are you waiting for? The sooner you
collect the fiendish hound that blocks me,
the sooner you'll start living in dog heaven!
Sincerely,
Harry Potter

- How is this revision different from the draft?
  What words have been changed?
  What phrases have been added?
  What clauses have been added?

- Words that have been changed: escaped (not "ran away"), get your mitts on (not "can have"), retire and live a yap-happy life (not "make more money"), fame would be a bone you could chew on for years and years (not "you will become famous").

- Appositive phrase that has been added: the oddest of all oddities.

- Prepositional phrases that have been added: from your sideshow, on one, from exploring the belly of Hogwarts School, at your carnival, at the mouth, at the creature, of all oddities, of displaying the three-headed beast, of the month, for years and years, in dog heaven.

- Gerund phrases that have been added: barring me, frothing at the mouth, displaying the three-headed beast.

- Infinitive phrases that have been added: to get a look at the creature, to retire and live a yap-happy life, to make enough money, to write a book.

- Adjective clause that has been added: that blocks me.

- Adverbial clauses that have been added: if you had a three-headed dog, the sooner you collect the fiendish hound.

Editing/Sharing: Check to see that your revision has commas, periods, apostrophes, and question marks in the right places. Check to see that all the words are spelled correctly. Share the poem by reading it aloud.

Assessment Form

____ The poem is persuasive: it attempts to convince someone to help a character from a story solve his or her problem.

____ The poem has a claim and three reasons; the reasons appeal to the self-interest of the person being persuaded.

____ The poem contains concrete, specific language.

____ Phrases and clauses are used effectively.

____ Transition words are used effectively.

____ The ideas and images in the poem fit together; they make sense together, and they work to support the main idea being expressed in the poem.

____ Mechanical, spelling, and punctuation errors have been avoided.

Writing Activity IV: "A Great Day" Poem

Prewriting: Make a list of characters or people from books or biographies you have read: Rapunzel, Cinderella, Harry Potter, George Washington, Charles Lindbergh, Wilma Rudolph.

■ Choose one and make a list of things that the character or person you have chosen would think would happen during a "great day." (Think of all the problems the character or person had and the kinds of things that would have made those problems go away or that would have made them easier to deal with.) For example, the Big Bad Wolf: a pork delivery service, all pig houses made of straw or sticks, a wolf pack, a battering ram, a wolf society for cheering on hungry wolves, pig-flavored toothpaste.

Drafting: pick three or four of your ideas from prewriting and use them in "A Great Day" poem. Begin your poem with the line, "I know it's going to be a great day when _____"

> I know it's going to be a great day when
> there's a pork delivery service,
> all pig houses are made of straw or sticks,
> I join a wolf pack,
> I get a battering ram for my birthday,
> I find pig-flavored toothpaste in the store,
> I am not misunderstood.

Revising: add more information to each line. Use strong nouns, verbs, and adjectives; also use phrases and clauses.

> I know it's going to be a day for happy howling when
>
> a pork delivery service offers me a free, lifetime certificate; a law is passed that all pig houses must be built of straw or sticks;
>
> I get a battering ram for my birthday—just in case I find a pig fortress, a horrible house of bricks, that won't shatter under the barrage of my breath;
>
> I win the "Best Breath Blaster" award at school;
>
> I find pig-flavored toothpaste and ham-flavored ice cream studded with bacon bits in the grocery store;
>
> blaming wolves for the world's woes fades away;
>
> both people and pigs no longer call me a cold, callous, crafty, crude carnivore!

■ How is the revision different from the draft?
What words have been changed?
What phrases have been added?
What clauses have been added?

■ Words that have been changed: built (not "made of"), cold, callous, crafty, crude carnivore (not "misunderstood").

■ Appositive phrase that has been added: a horrible house of bricks.

■ Gerund phrase that has been added: blaming wolves.

■ Prepositional phrases that have been added: for howling, for my birthday, of my breath, at school, with bacon bits, in the grocery store.

- Participial phrase that has been added: studded with bacon bits.

- Adjective clause that has been added: that won't shatter under the barrage of my breath.

- Adverbial clause that has been added: that all pig houses must be built of straw or sticks.

Editing/Sharing: Check to see that your revision has commas, periods, apostrophes, and question marks in the right places. Check to see that all the words are spelled correctly. Share the poem by reading it aloud.

Assessment Form

____ The poem describes a great day.

____ The poem gives specific examples of the aspects of a great day.

____ The ideas and images in the poem fit together; they make sense together, and they work to support the main idea being expressed in the poem.

____ The poem contains concrete, specific language.

____ Phrases and clauses are used effectively.

____ Transition words are used effectively.

____ Mechanical, spelling, and punctuation errors have been avoided.

Writing Activity V: A "Two-Voice" Poem

Prewriting: Make a list of characters from books or a list of people from biographies you have read. You can also make a list of animals or objects.

- Pick two people, characters, animals, places, etc. Make a database of facts for each. Put three or four facts under each category.

  ### Animal categories

habitat	attributes	actions
diet	enemies	life span

  ### People/character categories

childhood	abilities	what I like
what I don't like	friends	enemies
accomplishments	tasks or trials	setbacks

Drafting: Choose three or four categories to compare; choose a fact from each category. For example: I am Rapunzel, I am Rumpelstiltskin. (Describe actions, attributes, thoughts, feelings, etc.).

Actions:
I am Rapunzel: I live in a tower.
I am Rumpelstiltskin: I turn straw into golden thread.

Attributes:
I am Rapunzel: I have long hair.
I am Rumpelstiltskin: I have a short body.

Actions:
I am Rapunzel: I let down my hair so that the old woman can climb up to visit me.
I am Rumpelstiltskin: I give the queen three days to say my name.

Thoughts:

I am Rapunzel: I wonder if I'll ever leave this tower.
I am Rumpelstiltskin: I wonder if anyone will ever love me.

Revising: Replace weak or abstract nouns and verbs with ones that are concrete and vivid. Add phrases and clauses.

Actions:

I am Rapunzel: Pacing from window to window, wishing for wings, I seek escape, but the tower boxes me in.
I am Rumpelstiltskin: Sitting at the wheel, spinning straw into golden thread, I seek love, but I devise tricks instead.

Thoughts:

I am Rapunzel: I wonder about crowds, about swimming among a sea of people.
I am Rumpelstiltskin: I wonder about family, about hearing the sounds of children laughing.

Attributes:

I am Rapunzel: My tears can heal the blind.
I am Rumpelstiltskin: My magic can save the life of a weaver's daughter.

Accomplishments:

I am Rapunzel: I hacked my hair, weaved it into a rope, and slithered to freedom.
I am Rumpelstiltskin: I turned a girl into a queen, asked only for a child in return, and soared away in defeat when she spoke my name.

Desires:

I am Rapunzel: To hear the sounds of many voices, to walk among throngs of people is all I want.

I am Rumpelstiltskin: To love and to be loved is all I want.

■ How is the revision different from the draft?
   What words have been changed?
   What phrases have been added?
   What clauses have been added?

■ Words that have been changed: Pacing from window to window, wishing for wings, I seek escape, but the tower boxes me in (not "I live in a tower"); Sitting at the wheel, spinning straw into golden thread, I seek love, but I devise tricks instead (not "I turn straw into golden thread"); I hacked my hair, weaved it into a rope, and slithered to freedom (not "I let down my hair so that the old woman can climb up to visit me"); I turned a girl into a queen, asked only for a child in return, and soared away in defeat when she spoke my name (not "I give the queen three days to say my name").

■ Gerund phrases that have been added: swimming among a sea of people, hearing the sounds of children laughing.

■ Infinitive phrases that have been added: to hear the sounds of many voices, to walk among throngs of people, to love, to be loved.

■ Prepositional phrases that have been added: from window to window, for wings, about crowds, about swimming among a sea of people, about family, about hearing the sounds of children, of a weaver's daughter, into a rope, to freedom, into a queen, for a child in return, in defeat.

- Participial phrases that have been added: Pacing from window to window, wishing for wings, sitting at the wheel, spinning straw into golden thread.

- Adverbial clause that has been added: when she spoke my name.

Editing/Sharing: Check to see that your revision has commas, periods, apostrophes, and question marks in the right places. Check to see that all the words are spelled correctly. Share the poem by reading it aloud.

Assessment Form

____ The poem presents voices from two characters.

____ In the poem, each "voice" offers a different perspective on the same thing: a fact, an action, a thought, a feeling, etc.

____ The ideas and images in the poem fit together; they make sense together, and they work to support the main idea being expressed in the poem.

____ The poem contains concrete, specific language.

____ Phrases and clauses are used effectively.

____ Mechanical, spelling, and punctuation errors have been avoided.

Writing Activity VI: Imitation Poem—"The Eagle"

Read the following poem by Alfred, Lord Tennyson:

The Eagle
He clasps the crag with crooked hands;
Close to the sun in lonely lands,
Ringed with the azure world, he stands.

The wrinkled sea beneath him crawls,
He watches from his mountain walls,
And like a thunderbolt he falls.

Tell what you noticed about the poem. Consider how the poem is arranged, what special words it has, and what it is describing.

- Structure: the poem has two stanzas; each stanza has three lines.
  Line one describes what the eagle is doing.
  Lines two and three describe where the eagle is; these lines describe the eagle's environment.
  Line four describes the place beneath the eagle, what it is doing.
  Lines five and six describe two things the eagle does.

- Special words:
  clasps the crag with crooked hands (strong, concrete language and alliteration)
  ringed: surrounded by (strong verb)
  wrinkled: an unusual way to describe the ocean's surface (strong adjective)
  crawls: an unusual way to describe the ocean's movement (strong verb)
  like a thunderbolt: (strong comparison)

Prewriting:

■ Make a list of animals.

leopard frog, zebra, hummingbird, python, polar bear, mako shark, bottle-nosed dolphin, panther, wolf, mouse, butterfly, lemur, groundhog, sloth, etc.

■ Choose an animal. Put three or four facts about the animal (that you have researched) under each of the following categories.

habitat   attributes   actions
diet   enemies   life span

Drafting: Write a two-stanza poem, which is similar to Tennyson's, in which you describe an animal. Use facts you gathered from the listed categories. In the first stanza, tell what the animal is doing and where it is. In the second stanza, describe some aspect of the animal's world and tell what the animal does. Your poem does not need to rhyme.

Notice that the poem first describes where the animal is and ends with the animal's movement. The eagle perches, watches, falls.

EXAMPLE:

The Leopard Frog
He rests on the lily pad with comfort and ease;
Near the cattails in the pond
Surrounded by calm water he rests.

The pond is smooth and flat;
He watches from his green throne,
And like a cat he leaps.

Revising: Replace weak words with strong ones. Replace weak phrases or clauses with ones that are more precise.

The Leopard Frog
He lounges on the lily pad with yawning ease;
Near the cattails in a watery world
Surrounded by silence he sits.

Around him the pond holds its breath;
He gazes from his green throne,
And like a leopard he leaps.

■ How is the revision different from the draft?
What words have been changed?
What phrases have been added?
What clauses have been added?

■ Words that have been changed: lounges (not "rests"), yawning ease (not "comfort and ease"), watery world (not "in the pond"), silence (not "calm water"), sits (not "rests"), holds its breath (not "smooth and flat"), gazes (not "watches"), leopard (not "cat").

■ Alliteration: lounges–lily, watery–world, surrounded–silence–sits, gazes–green, like–leopard–leaps

- Prepositional phrases that have been used: on the lily pad; with yawning ease; near the cattails; in a watery world; by silence; around him; from his green throne; like a leopard.

- Participial phrase that has been used: surrounded by silence.

Editing/Sharing: Check to see that your revision has commas, periods, apostrophes, and question marks in the right places. Check to see that all the words are spelled correctly. Share the poem by reading it aloud.

Assessment Form

____ The poem describes an animal by following the structure of the model poem.

____ In the first stanza, the poem tells what the animal is doing and where it is.

____ In the second stanza, the poem describes some aspect of the animal's world and tells what the animal does.

____ The ideas and images in the poem fit together; they make sense together, and they work to support the main idea being expressed in the poem.

____ The poem contains concrete, specific language.

____ Phrases and clauses are used effectively.

____ Mechanical, spelling, and punctuation errors have been avoided.

Writing Activity VII: Imitation Poem—"The Argument of His Book"

Read the following poem by Robert Herrick:

The Argument of His Book

I sing of brooks, of blossoms, birds, and bowers,
Of April, May, of June, and July flowers.
I sing of Maypoles, hock carts, wassails, wakes,
Of bridegrooms, brides, and of their bridal cakes.
I write of youth, of love, and have access
By these to sing of cleanly wantonness.
I sing of dews, of rains, and piece by piece,
Of balm, of oil, of spice, and ambergris.
I sing of times trans-shifting, and I write
How roses first came red and lilies white.
I write of groves, of twilights, and I sing
The court of Mab and of the fairy king. . . .

Tell what you noticed about the poem. Consider how the poem is arranged, what special words it has, and what it is describing.

- Structure: the poem has one long stanza. Lines one, three, five, seven, nine, and eleven all begin with either "I sing" or "I write." Each of these is followed by specific things that Herrick is celebrating.

- Special words: blossoms, birds, and bowers, wassails, wakes (strong, concrete language and alliteration). What other special words do you see?

Prewriting: Make a list of things you could "sing about" or celebrate: bubble gum, pizza, new tennis shoes, summer, birthdays, bicycles, etc. Include some things that are unusual: how tadpoles become frogs, whales, cats in cardboard boxes, roller-coaster rides, balloons shooting through the air, the smell of popcorn, snow sledding, etc.

Drafting: Write a one-stanza poem (eight to ten lines), that is similar to Herrick's, in which you describe specific things that you celebrate. Your poem does not need to rhyme.

■ Begin each line with either "I sing," or "I write," or "I celebrate." Each of these should be followed by specific things that you are celebrating. Use the things from your prewriting list. End the poem with a line like, "I sing of these things and one day hope to have them all."

The Argument of My Song

I sing of the bubble gum I chew.

I sing of summer vacations away from school.

I sing of new tennis shoes on my feet.

I sing of tadpoles becoming frogs.

I sing of cats in cardboard boxes.

I sing of roller-coaster rides.

I sing of polar bears in the snow.

I sing of whales swimming in the ocean.

I sing of these things and one day hope to have them all.

Revising: Change nouns and verbs; add phrases and clauses to sharpen the ideas in the poem.

The Shape of My Song

I sing of pink bubble gum that I plop into my mouth to blow and pop.

I sing of summer vacations, of sun-soaked swimming pools perfect for belly flops.

I sing of the gleaming white tennis shoes hugging my feet.

I sing of tiny tadpoles stretching into fierce frogs.

I sing of crafty cats crouching in crinkled cardboard boxes.

I sing of roller coasters, of my stomach surging into my throat as I drop down, down, down.

I sing of shaggy polar bears lumbering across desolate ice packs.

I sing of wide whales sounding and singing in ocean depths.

I sing of these things and, one day, hope to have them all.

■ How is the revision different from the draft?

What words have been changed?

What phrases have been added?

What clauses have been added?

■ Words that have been changed: plop into my mouth to blow and pop (not "chew"), gleaming white (not "new"), stretching into (not "becoming"), lumbering across desolate ice packs (not "in the snow"), sounding and singing in ocean depths (not "swimming in the ocean").

■ Infinitive phrase that has been added: to blow and pop.

- Prepositional phrases that have been added: into my mouth, of sun-soaked swimming pools, for belly flops, into fierce frogs, in crinkled cardboard boxes, of my stomach, into my throat, in ocean depths, across desolate ice packs.

- Participial phrases that have been added: hugging my feet, stretching into fierce frogs, surging into my throat, lumbering across desolate ice packs, sounding and singing in ocean depths.

- Adjective clause that has been added: that I plop into my mouth to blow and pop.

Editing/Sharing: Check to see that your revision has commas, periods, apostrophes, and question marks in the right places. Check to see that all the words are spelled correctly. Share the poem by reading it aloud.

Assessment Form

____ The poem is a celebration of things, emotions, or ideas; it follows the structure of the model poem.

____ Each line begins with "I sing," or "I write," or "I celebrate." Each of these is followed by specific things that are celebrated.

____ The poem ends with a line like, "I sing of these things and one day hope to have them all."

____ The ideas and images in the poem fit together; they make sense together, and they work to support the main idea being expressed in the poem.

____ The poem contains concrete, specific language.

____ Phrases and clauses are used effectively.

____ Mechanical, spelling, and punctuation errors have been avoided.

Writing Activity VIII: Imitation Poem—"The Tyger"

Read the following poem by William Blake:

The Tyger
Tyger! Tyger! burning bright
In the forests of the night,
What immortal hand or eye
Could frame thy fearful symmetry?

In what distant deeps or skies
Burnt the fire of thine eyes?
On what wings dare he aspire?
What the hand dare seize the fire?

And what shoulder, & what art
Could twist the sinews of thy heart?
And, when thy heart began to beat,
What dread hand? & what dread feet?

What the hammer? what the chain?
In what furnace was thy brain?
What the anvil? what dread grasp
Dare its deadly terrors clasp?

When the stars threw down their spears,
And water'd heaven with their tears,
Did he smile his work to see?
Did he who made the Lamb make thee?

Tyger! Tyger! burning bright,
In the forests of the night,
What immortal hand or eye
Dare frame thy fearful symmetry?

Tell what you noticed about the poem. Consider how the poem is arranged, what special words it has, and what it is describing.

■ Structure: the poem has six four-line stanzas. Each stanza asks a question about the tiger. The questions ask how the tiger came to be, how it was put together, what it is made of.

■ Special words and phrases: frame thy fearful symmetry, on what wings dare he aspire, twist the sinews, stars threw down their spears.

Prewriting: Make a list of animals or work with the list you made for the poem "The Eagle."

leopard frog, zebra, hummingbird, python, polar bear, mako shark, bottle-nosed dolphin, panther, wolf, mouse, butterfly, lemur, groundhog, sloth, etc.

■ Choose an animal. Put three or four facts, which you have researched, about the animal under each of the following categories.

habitat   attributes   actions
diet   enemies   life span

■ Think of questions you can ask about the animal's habitat, attributes, actions, diet, enemies, or life span. The questions should focus on where the animal came from, how it came to be, where it got its parts, how it lives, why it lives where it does, why it eats what it does, and why it lives as long as it does. The questions can be silly or serious.

Drafting: Write a poem like Blake's. Your poem does not need to be as long as his; it can be from four to ten lines. It need not rhyme.

In your poem, ask questions about the animal. Don't give any answers. (You can write about more than one animal if you wish; just ask one or two questions about each animal.)

Black-Chinned Hummingbird
Hummingbird, where did you get your black neck?
Where did you learn to hover and fly backward?
How did you learn to fly so fast?
Why are your feathers bright in the sun?
Do you like other food besides nectar?
Why is your beak so long?
Why are you so small?

Revising: Change nouns and verbs; add phrases and clauses to sharpen the ideas in the poem.

Black-Chinned Hummingbird

Hummingbird, where did you get your dark collar?
   Did you buy a tiny turtleneck sweater?
Where did you learn to hover and fly backward?
   Did you take lessons from a helicopter?
How did you flit so fast through the air?
   Was your father a bolt of lightning?
Why do your feathers shine and shimmer in the sun?
   Do you wax and buff them every morning?
If you had teeth, what would you eat?
   Would you like to munch on dark chocolate?
Why is your beak so long and curved?
   Do you use it like a sword?
Why are you so small and explosive?
   Are you the feathery firecracker of the bird world?

■ How is the revision different from the draft?
What words have been changed?
What phrases have been added?
What clauses have been added?

■ Notice that each question has a follow-up question that asks for more information about something in the first question.

■ Words that have been changed: dark collar (not "black neck"), flit (not "fly"), shine and shimmer (not "bright"), if you had teeth, what would you eat (not "do you like other food besides nectar?").

■ Prepositional phrases that have been added: from a helicopter, through the air, on dark chocolate, of the bird world.

Editing/Sharing: Check to see that your revision has commas, periods, apostrophes, and question marks in the right places. Check to see that all the words are spelled correctly. Share the poem by reading it aloud.

Assessment Form

____ The poem asks questions to animals.

____ The questions are paired: the first question asks for information, the second question offers a speculative answer.

____ The ideas and images in the poem fit together; they make sense together, and they work to support the main idea being expressed in the poem.

____ The poem contains concrete, specific language.

____ Phrases and clauses are used effectively.

____ Mechanical, spelling, and punctuation errors have been avoided.

Writing Activity IX: Imitation Poem—"A Red, Red Rose"

Read the following stanza from a poem by Robert Burns:

O, my love is like a red, red rose,
   That's newly sprung in June:
O, my love is like the melody
   That's sweetly play'd in tune.

Tell what you noticed about the stanza. Consider how the stanza is arranged, what special words it has, and what it is describing.

■ Structure: Four lines. The first two lines compare love to a red, red rose. The second two lines compare love to a sweet melody.

■ Special words and phrases: red, red rose, newly sprung, sweetly play'd.

Prewriting: Make a list of emotions.

   love, hate, anger, fear, anxiety, boredom, joy, sadness, confusion, nervousness, etc.

■ Choose an emotion. Think of a time when you felt that emotion or saw someone else who felt that emotion. Make a clear picture in your memory.

Drafting: Use the following pattern to write about the emotion you have chosen.

   If _____ were an animal, it would be a _____ .
   If _____ were a plant, it would be a _____ .
   If _____ were a machine, it would be a _____ .
   If _____ were weather, it would be a _____ .
   If anger were an animal, it would be a rattlesnake.
   If anger were a plant, it would be poison ivy.
   If anger were a machine, it would be a jackhammer.
   If anger were weather, it would be a tornado.

■ What else do you imagine anger would be? There are lots of different ideas that will work.

Revising: Change nouns and verbs; add phrases and clauses.

   If anger were an animal, it would be a ruthless rattlesnake, rolled into a coil, ready to strike.
   If anger were a plant, it would be poison ivy itching for its next victim.
   If anger were a machine, it would be a jackhammer pounding the pavement.
   If anger were weather, it would be a tornado swirling through the countryside, tearing up trees, and tossing cars like they were toys.

■ How is the revision different from the draft?
   What words have been changed?
   What phrases have been added?
   What clauses have been added?

■ Prepositional phrases that have been added: into a coil, for its next victim, through the countryside.

■ Participial phrases that have been added: rolled into a coil, itching for its next victim, pounding the pavement, whirling through the countryside, tearing up trees, tossing cars like they were toys.

■ Infinitive that has been added: to strike.

■ Alliteration: ruthless-rattlesnake rolled-ready, pounding-pavement, tearing-trees-tossing-toys.

Editing/Sharing: Check to see that your revision has commas, periods, apostrophes, and question marks in the right places. Check to see that all the words are spelled correctly. Share the poem by reading it aloud.

Assessment Form

____ The poem compares emotions to concrete objects.

____ The ideas and images in the poem fit together; they make sense together, and they work to support the main idea being expressed in the poem.

____ The poem contains concrete, specific language.

____ Phrases and clauses are used effectively.

____ Mechanical, spelling, and punctuation errors have been avoided.

Writing Activity X: Imitation Poem—"I Wandered Lonely as a Cloud"

Read the following stanza by William Wordsworth:

I wandered lonely as a cloud
    That floats on high o'er vales and hills,
When all at once I saw a crowd,
    A host, of golden daffodils,
Beside the lake, beneath the trees
    Fluttering and dancing in the breeze.

Tell what you noticed about the stanza. Consider how the stanza is arranged, what special words it has, and what it is describing.

■ Structure: Six lines. Lines one and two compare the speaker to a lonely, floating cloud; lines three through six describe what the speaker discovers from his new perspective, from the perspective of imagining himself as a cloud. The stanza suggests, among other things, that when we use similes in our writing, we open ourselves to new perspectives and experiences.

■ Special words and phrases: vales, host, fluttering—and the double prepositions, "beside the lake, beneath the trees," which lead to the double participles, "fluttering and dancing."

Prewriting: Make a list of concrete nouns.

book, pen, hat, shoe, brick, chalk, banana, mug, frigate, horse, frog, poem, flashlight, microphone, lunchbox, snow cone, cotton candy, roller coaster, etc.

■ Choose one. Think of what the item you have chosen is like. Try to think of how the item is like other things. Consider the object's shape, size, color, texture, and purposes.

Example: a pen

shape	size	color	texture	purposes
long	finger	blue/black	smooth	write
slender	½" thick	red/green	hard	draw
round	straw-sized	purple	cool	communicate

■ Think of other objects that have some of the same qualities that you have listed: needle (slender), straw (long and round), paintbrush (draw/paint), ship (carries things), river (long, slender, blue)

Your object: _____

shape   size   color   texture   purposes

Drafting: Write a poem like Wordsworth's where you compare one thing to other things.

Use this pattern: a _____ is like a _____ .

In the first blank put the item you have chosen; in the second blank put what the item is like (use your data base of categories and facts here).

A pen is like a needle.

A pen is like a straw.

A pen is like a paintbrush.

A pen is like a ship.

A pen is like a flash flood.

Revising I: Change nouns; add phrases and clauses (add an adverbial clause beginning with "because"). Explain why or how your object is like the object you're comparing it to.

A pen is like a needle because I use it to sew my thoughts to words.

A pen is like a straw because it sucks the words out of my brain and lands them on the page.

A pen is like a paintbrush because I use it to paint my paper with words.

A pen is like a ship because it carries my words across the sea of paper.

A pen is like a flash flood because it lets my words flow onto the page.

Revising II: Change nouns; add phrases and clauses. Try to get rid of a few instances of "because"; change how the clause is written.

A pen is like a needle; with it, I stitch together words and thoughts.

A pen is like a straw because it sucks sloshy words out of my brain—that wet word tank—and drips them onto the page.

A pen is like a paintbrush; with it, I color my paper with word-art.

A pen is like a ship carrying my words across a flat white sea.

A pen is like a river because it lets my words gush onto the dry valley of the page.

■ How is revision I different from revision II?
What words have been changed?
What phrases have been added?
What clauses have been added?

■ Words that have been changed: stitch (not "sew"), drips (not "lands"), color (not "paint"), word-art (not "words), gush (not "flow").

■ Participial phrase that has been added: carrying my words.

■ Appositive phrase that has been added: that wet word tank.

Editing/Sharing: Check to see that your revision has commas, periods, apostrophes, and question marks in the right places. Check to see that all the words are spelled correctly. Share the poem by reading it aloud.

Assessment Form

____ The poem compares things.

____ Each line compares two things; reasons for the comparisons are also given.

____ The ideas and images in the poem fit together; they make sense together, and they work to support the main idea being expressed in the poem.

____ The poem contains concrete, specific language.

____ Phrases and clauses are used effectively.

____ Mechanical, spelling, and punctuation errors have been avoided.

Writing Extensions

Writing Extension I: *Making Unusual Connections*

Prewriting: Look at the following lists of words. Add five words to each side. (The modifiers should NOT go with the nouns.)

Words That Name (Nouns)	Words That Modify (Adjectives & Participial)
apple	ruptured
clock	shrill
mirror	tangled
spoon	steamy
bridge	gloomy
broom	shallow
weeping willow	heavy
shell	snarling
cloud	flat
horse	melting

_____	_____
_____	_____
_____	_____
_____	_____
_____	_____

■ Randomly choose five nouns and five modifiers. Do not try to make logical connections. Work swiftly. For example: broom–gloomy, mirror–melting, shell–shrill, cloud–tangled, bridge–snarling

Drafting: In a brief, free-verse poem, try to use as many of these pairs as you can. Ask yourself: what might they all have in common? where might they all be found?

■ Make a list of settings or objects that you can describe with your pairs of words.

Settings	Objects
house	oak chest
basement	bridge
beach	plank
castle	box
forest	map

■ Choose a setting or an object; use it as the basis for your writing.

Like a gloomy broom, under a sky tangled with clouds,
the ogre walked across the snarling bridge.
He heard a shell-shrill voice under the bridge.
The ogre looked; he was so happy he cried.
His eyes were like melting mirrors. He found his brother.

Revising: Can you add, delete, or change words? Can you add phrases or clauses?

> As gloomy as a broom without bristles
> beneath a cloud-tangled sky,
> the ogre trudged across
> the sagging, splintered bridge—the bridge creaked so loudly
> that it seemed to be snarling.
> A voice from below, as shrill as shell, called to the ogre.
> Overcome with happiness, the ogre wept, his eyes
> like melting mirrors, as he spotted his long-lost brother.

■ Words that have been changed/added: trudged (not "walked"), sagging, splintered, creaked, wept, long-lost.

■ Prepositional phrases: without bristles, from below, to the ogre, with happiness.

■ Infinitive phrase: to be snarling.

■ Adverbial clauses: that it seemed to be snarling, as he spotted his long-lost brother.

Editing/Sharing: Check to see that your revision has commas, periods, apostrophes, and question marks in the right places. Check to see that all the words are spelled correctly. Share the poem by reading it aloud.

Assessment Form

____ The poem offers unique word combinations.

____ The poem describes a character, actions, and a setting.

____ The ideas and images in the poem fit together; they make sense together, and they work to support the main idea being expressed in the poem.

____ The poem contains concrete, specific language.

____ Phrases and clauses are used effectively.

____ Mechanical, spelling, and punctuation errors have been avoided.

Writing Extension II: *Dream Poem*

Prewriting: Think of a dream you had. Write down where you were in the dream, when the dream happened, who else was in the dream, what you did, how you felt, and whether anything strange or unusual happened.

■ Where: on a bicycle on an empty street

■ When: at sunset

■ Who else: no one (at first), the green dogs and blue cows

■ What you did: riding the bike, looking for a way home, pedaling furiously

■ How you felt: nervous, afraid

■ Strange things: the bike goes by itself, I am at a birthday party

Drafting: Write a poem about the dream. In the first stanza, tell where and when the dream is happening. In the second stanza, tell what you are doing, why you are doing it, how you feel, and anything strange that happened.

> The street is empty.
> The sun is setting.
>
> I'm riding my bicycle and
> I'm trying to get home.
> I'm lost. I feel nervous.
> Suddenly a bunch of green dogs and blue cows
> start chasing me. I pedal faster.
> Then, I'm at a birthday party eating cake.

Revising: Can you add, delete, or change words? Can you add phrases or clauses? Because you're describing a dream, it doesn't have to "make sense"; it can be strange or even silly. In fact, you can even add things to the poem that were not in the original dream. Just try to paint a clear picture of the event.

> In my pedaling dream,
> the sun sinks into a dingy orange
> and leaves blow
> across a deserted street.
> I'm riding my bicycle, trying to get home.
> Lost, I feel my stomach drop
> like an elevator that doesn't stop.
> From out of nowhere, a pack of green dogs and herd of blue cows
> burst onto the street. They growl and moo after me.
> I pedal faster. My feet move as fast as a whirling fan.
> I hunch forward. Sweat stings my eyes.
> I turn a corner, and suddenly
> I'm at a birthday party. Surrounded by
> stuffed toy dogs, I eat blue cake.

■ Words that have been changed/added: in my pedaling dream, sun sinks into a dingy orange (not "sun is setting"); I feel my stomach drop like an elevator that doesn't stop (not "I feel nervous"); From out of nowhere, a pack green dogs and herd of blue cows burst onto the street. They growl and moo after me (not "a bunch of green dogs and blue cows start chasing me"); My feet move as fast as a whirling fan. I hunch forward. Sweat stings my eyes. Surrounded by stuffed toy dogs, I eat blue cake.

■ Prepositional phrases: into a dingy orange, across a deserted street, from out of nowhere, of green dogs, of blue cows, onto the street, after me, by stuffed toy dogs.

■ Participial phrase: trying to get home, surrounded by stuffed toy dogs.

■ Adjective clause: that doesn't stop.

Editing/Sharing: Check to see that your revision has commas, periods, apostrophes, and question marks in the right places. Check to see that all the words are spelled correctly. Share the poem by reading it aloud.

Assessment Form

____ The poem describes a dream.

____ In the first stanza, the poem tells where and when the dream is happening.

____ In the second stanza, the poem tells what you are doing, why you are doing it, how you feel, and anything strange that happened.

____ The ideas and images in the poem fit together; they make sense together, and they work to support the main idea being expressed in the poem.

____ The poem contains concrete, specific language.

____ Phrases and clauses are used effectively.

____ Mechanical, spelling, and punctuation errors have been avoided.

Writing Extension III: *Who Am I?*

Prewriting: Think of things you like, things you like to do, things you don't like, and things you don't like to do. Add more things to these lists:

Things I Like
bubble gum
gooey cheese pizza
scary stories
frogs
chocolate milk

_____

_____

_____

_____

_____

Things I Like to Do
fly kites
play baseball
pretend I'm a superhero
ride roller coasters
throw water balloons

_____

_____

_____

_____

_____

Things I Don't Like
canned peas
sardines
the flu
allergy shots
mean dogs

_____

_____

_____

_____

Things I Don't Like to Do
fill out worksheets for homework
clean my room
go to the dentist
go into the basement alone
go to bed early

_____

_____

_____

_____

Drafting: Pick some things from each list and use them in a "Who Am I?" poem. In the poem tell who you are, but use the things from your list. The things from your list describe what you like and don't like—and these things tell a lot about who you are. In the first stanza, tell who you are; in the second, tell who you are not.

Who Am I?
I'm chocolate milk.
I'm flying kites.
I'm throwing water balloons.
I'm scary stories.
I'm frogs.
I'm roller coasters.

I'm not worksheets for homework.
I'm not a trip to the dentist.
I'm not a clean room.
I'm not allergy shots.
I'm not sardines.

Revising: Can you add, delete, or change words? Can you add phrases or clauses? Try to give more information about each thing in each line.

Who Am I?
I'm chocolate milk moustache.
I'm flying kites on cool, windy days.
I'm throwing water balloons on sticky summer afternoons.
I'm scary stories told in whispers on stormy nights.
I'm frogs submarining through secret ponds.
I'm roller coasters rocketing through space.
I'm not worksheets for homework, the ones that make my brain
    feel like a tiger pacing in a cage.
I'm not a trip to the dentist, where my mouth feels
    like a candy bar melting in the sun.
I'm not a clean room, a place too perfect to live.
I'm not allergy shots, weekly spikes in the arm.
I'm not sardines, those dead fish in a coffin can.

- Appositive phrases: the ones that make my brain feel like a tiger pacing in a cage, those dead fish in a coffin can.

- Infinitive: to live.

- Prepositional phrases: on cool, windy days, on sticky summer afternoons, on stormy nights, through space, in a cage, in the sun, in the arm, in a coffin can.

- Participial phrases: submarining through secret ponds, rocketing through space, melting in the sun.

- Adjective clauses: that make my brain feel like a tiger pacing in a cage, where my mouth feels like a candy bar melting in the sun.

Editing/Sharing: Check to see that your revision has commas, periods, apostrophes, and question marks in the right places. Check to see that all the words are spelled correctly. Share the poem by reading it aloud.

Assessment Form

____ The poem tells who you are and who you are not; it uses items from your prewriting lists in each stanza.

____ The ideas and images in the poem fit together; they make sense together, and they work to support the main idea being expressed in the poem.

____ The poem contains concrete, specific language.

____ Phrases and clauses are used effectively.

____ Mechanical, spelling, and punctuation errors have been avoided.

Writing Extension IV: Colorful Writing 1

Prewriting: Think of ten to fifteen colors: green, blue, red, yellow, etc.

Choose one: green

Think of fifteen to twenty things that are the color you have chosen. Use concrete nouns (nouns that stand for things you can see, hear, touch, taste, and/or smell): a frog, summer grass, leaves, a grass snake, a shirt, rotten eggs, an emerald, a gremlin's skin, a stormy sky, a "go" light (the green part of a stoplight), a cat's eyes, lime jello, broccoli, lettuce, spinach, mold, the glow-in-the-dark face of a watch, a cactus, a parrot's wings, a dollar bill, peas, a shamrock, an alligator, a dragon, a praying mantis, etc.

Drafting: Choose five or six green things and write about them using this pattern:

What is _____ ? _____ is:

What Is Green?
Green is:
a frog
summer grass
a cat's eyes
a dollar bill
a gremlin's face

Revising: Tell more about each thing you wrote about in your draft. Add adjectives, phrases, and clauses.

What Is Green?
Green is:
a lumpy bullfrog, the emperor of the pond, perched on a lily pad, croaking rough music across his watery kingdom,
soft summer grass swaying, catching secret whispers of wind,
a cat's eyes peering out into the dark from inside the deep dark of a cardboard box,
a dollar bill crumpled in the pocket of a pair of jeans about to be tossed into the churning washing machine,
a gremlin's face after he gulped a dozen rotten eggs.

■ Appositive phrase: the emperor of the pond.

■ Infinitive phrase: to be tossed.

■ Prepositional phrases: of the pond, on a lily pad, across his watery kingdom, of wind, into the dark, from inside the deep dark, of a cardboard box, in the pocket, of a pair, of jeans, about to be tossed, into the churning washing machine.

■ Participial phrases: perched on a lily pad, croaking rough music, catching secret whispers, peering out into the dark, crumpled in the pocket.

■ Adjective clause: after he gulped a dozen rotten eggs.

Editing/Sharing: Check to see that your revision has commas, periods, apostrophes, and question marks in the right places. Check to see that all the words are spelled correctly. Share the poem by reading it aloud.

Assessment Form

____ The poem describes a color.

____ The poem compares one color to a series of concrete objects—those objects (and actions) represent or exemplify the color.

____ The ideas and images in the poem fit together; they make sense together, and they work to support the main idea being expressed in the poem.

____ The poem contains concrete, specific language.

____ Phrases and clauses are used effectively.

____ Mechanical, spelling, and punctuation errors have been avoided.

Writing Extension V: Colorful Writing II

Prewriting: Think of ten to fifteen colors: green, blue, red, yellow, etc.

Choose one: Blue.

Think of ten to fifteen things that are the color you have chosen—but these things should be things that you can HEAR, not see. You'll have to use your imagination to connect a color to things you can hear. The things that you can hear should somehow represent the color you have chosen. Start by listing things that make noises or things you associate with other things that make noise: waves, the rain, ink pen, fire, music, tears, ice, a window or mirror, the moon, thunder, a bruise, etc.

Drafting: Choose five or six blue things and write about them using this pattern:

What is _____? _____ is the sound of:

What Is Blue?
Blue is the sound of:
rain
an ink pen
the moon
ice
music

Revising: Describe the sound of each thing you wrote about in your draft. Add adjectives, phrases, and clauses.

What Is Blue?
Blue is the sound of:
>   rain dropping, plopping, flopping into puddles,
>   an ink pen scratching across a white page,
>   the moon spinning solo in the shadowy sky,
>   ice melting on a steamy, summer sidewalk,
>   a violin crying, weeping tears of tunes.

■ Prepositional phrases: into puddles, across a white page, in the shadowy sky, on a steamy, summer sidewalk.

■ Participial phrases: dropping, plopping, flopping into puddles; scratching across a white page; spinning solo in the shadowy sky; melting on a steamy, summer sidewalk; crying, weeping tears of tunes.

Editing/Sharing: Check to see that your revision has commas, periods, apostrophes, and question marks in the right places. Check to see that all the words are spelled correctly. Share the poem by reading it aloud.

Assessment Form

____ The poem describes a color.

____ The poem compares one color to a series of concrete sounds—those sounds represent or exemplify the color.

____ The poem begins with a question and offers an extended answer.

____ The ideas and images in the poem fit together; they make sense together, and they work to support the main idea being expressed in the poem.

____ The poem contains concrete, specific language.

____ Phrases and clauses are used effectively.

____ Mechanical, spelling, and punctuation errors have been avoided.

Writing Extension VI: *The Poetry of Names*

Prewriting:

■ Generate a list of names; for example, Rapunzel, Snow White, Sleeping Beauty, Jack.

■ Generate a list of noises unrelated to the names—some made by mechanical devices, some made by natural occurrences. Use a noun-participle combination.

  Examples of noises made by mechanical devices: clock ticking, ball bouncing, computer humming

  Examples of noises made by natural occurrences: wind blowing, water gurgling

Drafting:

■ Choose a name and a sound that corresponds to it (do not use "logic" here).

  Example: Rapunzel = the wind sighing

■ Write five lines using this pattern: a name, a concrete sound (noun + participle), and a simile in each line.

■ A simile is a figure of speech that compares two unlike things, and is introduce by "like" or "as." Similes often compare an abstract noun to a concrete noun. "My love is like a red, red rose." Her anger was as powerful as a snarling bear. I was so sad that I felt like a dead-end sign on a forgotten road.

Examples:

Rapunzel sounds like the wind sighing.

Red Riding Hood sounds like a hummingbird humming.

Jack sounds like a pen writing.

Snow White sounds like a child sleeping.

Harry sounds like a hit baseball.

Revising:

■ Add a prepositional phrase to each line.

Commonly Used Prepositions

about	below	for	throughout
above	beneath	from	to
across	beside	in	toward
after	besides	into	under
against	between	like	underneath
along	beyond	of	until
amid	but ("except")	off	unto
among	by	on	up
around	concerning	over	upon
at	down	past	with
before	during	since	within
behind	except	through	without

■ A group of words may act as a preposition:

on account of   in spite of
along with   together with

■ A preposition introduces the phrase. The noun or pronoun that ends the prepositional phrase is the OBJECT of the preposition that introduces the phrase. Prepositional phrases show relationships and give information.

■ Change the verb (or verb form); choose one that is vivid, concrete, and appeals to the senses.

■ Add descriptive details (adjectives, participial phrases . . .)

■ Break the lines to emphasize words, images, and/or ideas.

EXAMPLE:

Rapunzel sounds like a twilight breeze
sighing through a forest of leaf-dappled trees.
Red Riding Hood sounds like a hummingbird humming
away from a clutch of oleanders.
Jack sounds like a pen scratching across
a blank sheet of paper.
Snow White sounds like
the sigh of a child drifting into sleep.
Harry sounds like a baseball crashing
through the font window of a abandoned house.

Editing:

■ Check spelling and punctuation.

■ Check sentence structure (noun/verb agreement).

Sharing:

■ Read your poem.

Assessment Form

____ Each line has a simile that compares a name to a sound.

____ Each line has a noun–participle combination.

____ Each line has a prepositional phrase.

____ Concrete language. Vivid verbs.

____ No mechanical errors.

Ideas for Writing in the Content Areas

Just as students use the writing process for creating and crafting poems, so, too, should they use the process to write across the curriculum in different forms or genres. Here are some sample activities that will enable students to write about various nonfiction topics.

Writing about a Nonfiction Topic Using an Alliterative Pattern

Step One: Prewriting

1. Choose a topic: a person, place, animal, event, object, etc.

   Examples: Thomas Edison, Mount Rushmore, bullfrog, building of the Great Wall of China, hot air balloon

2. Choose a letter that does not begin the word you have chosen

   Example: bullfrog / the letter *F*

3. List words that begin with that letter, words that might also pertain to the character or object (consulting a dictionary may be helpful):

   Example: *F* Words for bullfrog: *floats, fast, flick, free, furtive*

Step Two: Drafting

Use this sentence-slotting pattern to write an alliterative sentence about the character or object you have chosen:

_____ is for _____ because _____.

DEFINITION: alliteration
Alliteration refers to the repetition of the same sounds at the beginning of a series of words.

1. In the first blank place a letter.

2. In the second blank place the name of the character (or object) that does not begin with the letter in the first blank.

3. In the third blank give an explanation, which may be words, a phrase, or a sentence; the explanation must contain words that begin with the letter in the first blank and must also contain "correct" information about the character.

   Example: *F* is for bullfrog because it flicks its tongue at feeble insects.

Step Three: Revising

■ Delete weak verbs, adverbs, and adjectives; replace them with stronger ones.

■ Strive to create a sentence that vividly and imaginatively describes your topic.

■ Add phrases and clauses.

■ The sentence should also offer correct information about the topic.

Step Four: Editing

■ Is the sentence complete and not a run-on sentence or fragment?

■ Are pronouns used correctly?

■ Are words spelled correctly?

■ Is proper punctuation used: commas, semicolons, apostrophes?

Example: **F** is for **bullfrog** because it **frequently** and **furtively floats** just beneath the **flat** surface of a lily-pad covered pond, and it **flicks** its **flypaper** tongue, **faster** than the **flash** of a **firefly**, at **feeble** insects that are **foolish** enough to **fly** or land nearby. After **finding** its **fill** of insect-**food**, the bullfrog becomes a *fullfrog*.

Step Five: Sharing/Publishing

■ Read your sentence(s) aloud.

Writing about Frogs (or a person, animal, or object, or place): Alternative Acrostic Poems

Begin with a database about your topic. Place facts beneath the following headings: *attributes, abilities, diet, lifespan, habitat, enemies*. Write acrostic poems about your topic.

1. Answer the questions who, what, when, where, why, how.

   where: F requently found in lily-pad-covered ponds.
   who: R apid flycatcher, spring loaded, ready for action.
   when: O n a warm spring day leaves its hibernation house in the pond's muddy bottom.
   why: G reen is the predominate color, which protects the frog from predators.

2. Use adjectives and/or alliteration.

   F ast, freedom-loving, frequently unseen
   R esonant, relaxed, royal
   O scillating, open-eyed, operatic
   G reen, gleaming, gravel-voiced

3. Use similes and/or metaphors.

   F ast as the flash of a firefly as they snap insects with their sticky tongues
   R ocketeers of the amphibian world, with arcing leaps, from pad to pad
   O pera stars croaking on lily-pad stages beneath the moon's spotlight
   G raceful as green gazelles as they spring from the bank to plop into the pond

Writing about Two Animals with a Contrast Pattern

Step One: Prewriting

Choose two animals. Create databases for each. Use these headings; be sure to put at least five concrete details beneath each heading.

attributes   actions   habitat   food   enemies   "is like . . . "

Step Two: Drafting

Use the following pattern to write about the animals:

If I were a _____ , I'd _____

and I'd _____ ,

but I wouldn't _____

because a _____ does that.

Example: If I were an alligator I'd have lots of teeth, and I'd move fast, but I wouldn't be able to run a long time because a wolf does that.

Step Three: Revising

Add more details to each slot. Use stronger verbs and/or figurative language. Use phrases and clauses.

Example: If I were an alligator, I'd have over eighty sharp teeth like little daggers lining my mouth, and I'd be able to blast out of the water like a rocket, but I wouldn't be able to lope all night long if I had to because a wolf does that.

Step Four: Editing

Check spelling and punctuation.

Step Five: Sharing/Publishing

Read your pattern aloud.

Writing about People, Things, or Animals: So You Want to Be

Start with a database:

habitat   physical features   abilities   diet   enemies   life-span   amazing facts

So you want to be (a person, animal, place, or thing)
You'll have to make your home in
and you'll have to have these three physical features
and you'll have to be able to do these two things
There are two good things about being
which are:
but there are two bad things about being
which are:
but the greatest thing about being
is

EXAMPLE:

So you want to be a *bullfrog*.

You'll have to make your home in ponds, lakes, streams, or rivers;

and you'll have to have these three physical features: two sharp eyes on the top of your head, long strong springy back legs, and a glue-covered tongue;

and you'll have to be able to do these two things: make croaking music at night and hibernate in the mud during the winter.

There are two good things about being a bullfrog, which are: you'll be the biggest frog in the pond and you'll be able to have fast-food meals when you zap bugs with your glue-tongue,

but there are two bad things about being a bullfrog, which are: horrible humans will want you for your back legs and you must always stay near water (you'll never live in the desert!),

but the greatest thing about being a bullfrog is that you will be the lily-pad flying star of the Caldecott Award-Winning picture book *Tuesday!*

The Five Good Things Pattern

Write about frogs (or anything else you have researched) using this pattern:

There are _____ good things about _____ .

They are: (first brainstorm a long list of possible ideas, choose the right number, list them, and use strong, concrete language).

- First, pick a topic: animal, person, place, thing.

- Create a database of facts about the topic (use only those categories that apply): attributes, abilities, origin, special features, talents, accomplishments, friends, enemies, ordeals, etc.

- Choose five facts from five different categories.

- Explain why each fact is "good." Use figurative language where possible. Also use concrete, specific language; use phrases and clauses.

Example: There are five good things about *frogs*. They are:

1. Frogs are wrapped in many different colors: green, blue, gold, and red, to name a few. Frogs are so colorful that they are living jewels.

2. Frogs are nature's barometers: when they are healthy they let you know that the air and water where they live are clean. When they get sick, though, they let you know that the air and water are polluted.

3. Frogs are powerful creatures! They can perform great leaps in a single bound. If a frog were the size of a human being, it could leap over ninety feet in a single spring.

4. Some frogs are fantastic. The Grey Tree Frog can actually freeze like a piece of ice and then thaw out to live again!

5. Frogs are the only animals that can "croak" every night and still keep on living!

Writing about a Nonfiction Topic Using an Informational Paragraph

Step One: Prewriting

Choose a topic: person or animal.

　　Example: armadillo

　　Create a database.

　　　　Animal: attributes　　actions　　habitat　　food　　enemies　　"is like . . ."

　　　　Person: personality traits　　attributes　　background (where and when)
　　　　　　　　talents　　trials/tests　　accomplishments

Step Two: Drafting

1. Choose a general word to describe the animal: *timid*.

2. Tell what the animal does that exemplifies the general word: When danger threatens, some species are able to roll up into tight round balls, with nothing showing but the thick, hard plates on their backs. It has short legs, but when alarmed it can run with considerable speed.

3. Tell how the animal does things: The animal's digging claws enable it to bury itself in an incredibly short time.

4. Use a simile or metaphor to describe the animal: Jointed plates, which cover the back and sides of the animal, look like the armor worn by medieval knights.

5. Tell what the animal is not: The armadillo is not ferocious like a badger.

Step Three: Revising

Use the items from the drafting stage in a paragraph. Begin with a topic sentence that contains one word that will tell something essential about the animal (or person). Use facts and explanations of those facts to support the idea in the topic sentence. Be sure to use sentence variety (create sentences with a variety of phrases and clauses); use transition words.

EXAMPLE:

Armadillos are *timid* creatures. Even though they resemble medieval knights because they wear an armor of joined plates, they do not like to fight. For example, armadillos feed on insects, worms, roots, fruits, and even carrion; in fact, they so timid that they never attack animals even as small as a mouse for a meal. Armadillos also reveal their timidity when they are attacked by a wolf or a mountain lion. Rather than scratch and bite their enemies the way a ferocious badger would, most armadillos roll up into tight round balls with nothing showing but the thick, hard plates on their backs. Others run away on their short, swift legs and then use their sharp claws to burrow quickly into the ground. Once inside the safety of the burrow, armadillos will use their keen hearing to listen for further danger. Despite being timid, however, armadillos know how to survive.

The Contrast Paragraph

Step One: Prewriting

Create databases for two animals. Use these headings; be sure to list at least five concrete details beneath each heading.

attributes   actions   habitat   food   enemies   is like . . .

Step Two: Drafting

■ Create a contrast paragraph in which you discuss the differences between two animals, places, people, or things. Example of block method:

The Great Owlet Moth and the Walking Stick are different in size and ability. The Great Owlet Moth has a body the size of a golf ball and a twelve-inch wingspan. In addition, the Great Owlet Moth can use its natural colors to hide in trees. It also is able to "hear" the radar of bats; it uses its great hearing to get away from them. By contrast, the Walking Stick's body is as skinny as a toothpick even though it is ten inches long. Unlike the Great Owlet Moth. the Walking Stick cannot fly, and it cannot hear the radar of bats. It can only climb on its four, slow legs.

■ Choose two or three categories to contrast. Choose one or two details from each category.

■ Create a contrast paragraph; use first-person point of view and divergent thinking. Begin with a topic sentence that asserts a preference for being one animal. Contrast at least two different categories that pertain to both animals—be sure to support the topic sentence. Give details for each category; follow each detail with a discussion that supports the assertion in the topic sentence.

■ Example of point-by-point method (contrasting the Great Owlet Moth and the Walking Stick):

I'd rather be a Great Owlet Moth than a Walking Stick. Although the Walking Stick is the longest of all insects, the Great Owlet Moth is one of the biggest. I think it would be much more fun to spread my twelve-inch wings and fly through a South American rain forest at dusk than have to strain to move my ten-inch, skinny body in a wobbly motion as I walked up a tree limb in Australia. Also, while the Great Owlet Moth and the Walking Stick can both hide themselves by blending into the trees upon which they are perched, a Great Owlet Moth can do something that the Walking Stick cannot. If I were a Walking Stick and was spotted by a hungry lizard, all I could do would be to hope to blend into the matching bark. But if I were a Great Owlet Moth I could blend into the background and I could detect the high-pitched "radar" sounds of bats and dart away to safety before they detected me. So I'd rather be a Great Owlet Moth than a walking stick.

Step Three: Revising

■ Add more concrete details in the form of participial phrases, infinitive phrases, absolute phrases, appositive phrases, prepositional phrases.

■ Change simple sentences into complex sentences with adjective clauses, adverbial clauses, or noun clauses.

■ Use stronger verbs. Use transitional words: although, but, by contrast, however, on the other hand, unlike, whereas, while.

■ Create a stronger voice—use personal observations. Be sure the topic sentence states the categories to be contrasted. Also be sure to discuss all facts and relate them to the topic idea.

Step Four: Editing

- Check spelling and punctuation. Make sure all sentences are complete sentences.

- Make sure all ideas connect.

EXAMPLE:

Even though both bugs are pretty cool, I'd rather be a Great Owlet Moth than a Walking Stick for two reasons: attributes and ability. Although the Walking Stick is the longest of all insects, the Great Owlet Moth is one of the biggest. I think it would be much more fun to spread my twelve-inch wings and gracefully wing my way through a South American rain forest at dusk—sometimes even being mistaken for a small, grey-brown owl!—rather than have to strain to move my ten-inch, skinny body in a wobbly, choppy, rocking motion as I walked up a tree limb in Australia (I think the other bugs would laugh at me and call me names like "wobble-walker" or "brittle-branch-body"). Even more important than attributes, however, is ability. While the Great Owlet Moth and the Walking Stick can both hide themselves by blending into the trees upon which they are perched, a Great Owlet Moth has a secret weapon that the Walking Stick does not. For instance, if I were a Walking Stick and was spotted by a hungry lizard, all I could do would be to "make like a stick," hug a tree branch, and hope to blend into the matching bark. On the other hand, if I were a Great Owlet Moth, I could use my camouflage to blend into the background and I could use my tiny, secret ears to actually detect the high-pitched "radar" sounds of bats—my enemies!—and dart away to safety before they detected me. So you can see, there are at least two distinct advantages to being a Great Owlet Moth rather than a Walking Stick.

Writing a Character Analysis/Personality Trait Paragraph

The five essential components of a character analysis/personality trait analysis paragraph are:

1. A topic sentence that contains one general idea—one aspect of personality. Here are some possible adjectives to use.

able	blunt	lucky	open-minded	frantic
sensitive	courageous	trustworthy	doubtful	angry
agreeable	giving	defeated	vivacious	thrilled
confident	gentle	inquisitive	selfish	intolerant
cranky	fragile	graceful	mysterious	mean
fierce	happy	secretive	tense	curious
determined	clever	persuasive	_____	_____

2. A restriction/exemplification sentence that narrows the focus of the topic sentence and offers one incident from the story as an example of the general idea in the topic sentence.

3. A quotation that relates directly to the incident mentioned in step 2.

4. A discussion that shows how the quotation exemplifies the idea in the topic sentence.

5. A concluding sentence that restates the topic sentence.

Choose a character from fiction or an actual person. If you choose a person, read about him or her and then write a paragraph that analyzes one aspect of the character's personality.

EXAMPLE:

1. Hamlet frequently experienced a sense of doubt. (topic sentence)

2. For example, when confronted with the specter who claimed to be his father the king, Hamlet experienced intense doubt. He could not decide if the ghost who claimed to be his father was an agent sent by the devil to lead him to death or a spirit from heaven who would offer him a divine gift. (restriction/transition sentences that offer an incident from the play)

3. In expressing this doubt, Hamlet said to the ghost in act 1, scene 4, "Be thou a spirit or a goblin . . . / Be thy intents wicked, or charitable, / Thou com'st in such a questionable shape / That I will speak to thee." (direct quotation from the play)

4. By stating that he thought the apparition's intents could either be "wicked or charitable," Hamlet indicated that he could not decide the truth of the matter. Thus, in his experience with the ghost, Hamlet felt a great doubt that shook both his mind and his spirit. (discussion)

5. This double doubt influenced and ultimately shaped his actions for the rest of the play. (concluding sentence)

Multi-Modal Character/Person Analysis Paragraph

Discuss the personality trait of a literary character or a real person.

Step One: Prewriting

■ Choose a character or person.

■ List seven to ten general/abstract words (other than "good," "bad,") that may properly describe the character's/person's personality.

■ Choose one word, define it (give the dictionary definition), and exemplify it by using each of the following five "modes": action, interpretive, gossip, relational, and *via negativa*.

EXAMPLE:

1. Character: Rumplestiltskin

2. Seven to ten general/abstract words that describe Rumplestiltskin's personality: sly, swift, enigmatic, magical, patient, single-minded, secretive, nimble.

3. One character trait: enigmatic.
   Definition: puzzling, ambiguous, unexplainable, or inexplicable

Step Two: Drafting

Write about the character using the five modes.

1. Action Mode: two things the character did that demonstrate the trait (enigmatic). First, Rumplestiltskin spun straw into golden thread without explaining how he was able to do so. Second, Rumpelstiltskin would not tell the Queen his name, but made her guess; the reasons for this are a mystery; that is, they are enigmatic.

2. Interpretive Mode: a simile or a metaphor that reveals the trait. Rumplestiltskin is like a door hinge because he opened the strange world of magic to the weaver's daughter.

3. Gossip Mode: what another character says (or might say) about the character that reveals the trait. "Even after all these years, I still don't understand where that little man came from or who he was—he said so very little. But what puzzles me most is his name: what mother in her right mind would give her son a bizarre name like 'Rumplestiltskin'? I mean, what kind of name is Rumplestiltskin? What does it mean?" (Queen to her son long after the "Stiltskin Incident").

4. Relational Mode: who or what the character is like. Rumplestiltskin is like the boy-artist in "The Boy Who Drew Cats" because they both possessed inexplicable abilities: Rumplestiltskin was able to ride on a wooden cooking spoon and the boy could draw cats that came to life in the dark.

5. *Via Negativa* Mode: what the character is not—that is, what trait that he does not possess that is the opposite of the one you are describing. Although Rumplestiltskin saved the weaver's daughter from three dangerous predicaments, he was, in the end, no Prince Charming—a character whose actions and intentions were clear and straightforward.

Step Three: Revising

Using words, phrases, clauses, revise. Strive for clarity and specificity.

Step Four: Editing

Check your writing for mechanical errors.

Step Five: Sharing/Publishing

Read your work aloud.

EXAMPLE:

The Queen is talking to her son years after the Rumplestiltskin episode:

What was he like, you ask? In a word, he was enigmatic. Let me tell you what I mean. Did you know that he could spin straw into golden thread? Yes, he really could! And even though I asked him repeatedly, he would not explain to me how he did it. I can't begin to tell you how frustrating it was not to know, especially after he left, and the king, your father, began demanding that I whip up more golden thread! But that's another story....

As I think about it now, I suppose that Rumplestiltskin reminds me of a door hinge because he opened the strange world of magic to me, a world that I still think of. Strange, but he also reminds me of that boy-artist from Japan who also possessed inexplicable abilities: just as Rumplestiltskin was able to ride a wooden cooking spoon, the boy, so I am told, could draw cats that came to life in the dark. Amazing.

Another thing about Rumplestiltskin that I don't understand is why he would not tell the me his name, why he made me guess. I suppose I'll never know. And I still don't know where he came from or who he was; he said so very little. But what puzzles me most is his name: I mean, what mother in her right mind would give her son a bizarre name like 'Rumplestiltskin'? Finally, I must say that although Rumplestiltskin did save me from a terrible predicament, he was, in the end, no Prince Charming—a man whose actions and intentions are clear and straightforward.

And by the way, dear Agamemnosticies, now that the king, your father, is no longer with us, I have taken the liberty of inviting this prince over for dinner....

Biographical Writing: Who Is the Real Walter Frederick Morrison?

Read the following; see if you can deduce who the real Morrison is.

Reading Parts: Host, Walter Frederick Morrison #1, Walter Frederick Morrison #2, Walter Frederick Morrison #3

Host: Welcome to "Whose Tale Is True?" Each of our three guests claims to be Walter Frederick Morrison, the inventor of the Frisbee. Only one, however, is telling the complete truth. It is up to you to decide who is the real Walter Frederick Morrison. Now let's meet our guests. Welcome. Can you tell us something about yourselves?

Walter Frederick Morrison #1: I am a school teacher in Butte, Montana; I teach physics.

Walter Frederick Morrison #2: I am a self-styled inventor; one of my most famous inventions is the zipper, which I invented in 1943.

Walter Frederick Morrison #3: I am the son of the inventor of a new kind of car headlight.

Host: What led you to invent the Frisbee? And how did you come up with the name, Frisbee?

Walter Frederick Morrison #1: One day in class I was demonstrating an experiment. I wanted to show my students the principles of aerodynamics, so I took a heavy paper plate and flung it across the room. Later that day, I saw my students outside flinging paper plates. The idea then hit me: I had "invented" a new form of recreation. I called the Wham-O Company and sold them on the idea. The name, Frisbee, comes from Latin: fris (from fribere)—to fling, and bee (from beetelen)—plate.

Walter Frederick Morrison #2: I have hundreds of inventions. And I like to wear flat, straw hats. One day as I was leaving my laboratory, the wind blew my hat off my head. Astonished, I watched my hat sail away from me. When I caught up with my hat, I picked it up and then flung it into the breeze. I did this several times. And then I knew I had it: a new invention! I went back into my lab, worked on a design, and created a plastic "flat hat" for throwing—or frisbee. The next day I took my invention to the Wham-O Company and sold it to them for $100,000. The name, Frisbee, came from my maternal grandfather: Charles J. Frisbee, a man I greatly admired.

Walter Frederick Morrison #3: I loved watching science fiction movies in the 1950s; my favorites were ones about flying saucers. Because the movies were so popular, I decided to try and "cash in" on the flying saucer craze. I invented a plastic "flying saucer," one that kids could throw to each other. I sold the "saucer" to the Wham-O Company. The name, Frisbee, comes from the Frisbie Pie Company in Bridgeport, Connecticut. It seems that students at Yale University used to toss Frisbie pie tins to one another.

Host: In what year did you invent the frisbee?

Walter Frederick Morrison #1: 1961.

Walter Frederick Morrison #2: 1949.

Walter Frederick Morrison #3: 1957.

Host: Now it is time to decide which of our guests is the real Walter Frederick Morrison. We will vote by a show of hands. Is it number one? Is it number two? Is it number three? Now for the moment you have all been waiting for. Will the real Walter Frederick Morrison, the inventor of the frisbee, please step forward.

Walter Frederick Morrison #3 steps forward.

How to Write Your Own Script

The objective is for the students to research the life of a person and report their findings in the form of a script. To get students started, invite them to select a person they want to investigate (you may want to furnish a list of persons from which students can choose). As the students read about the person they have chosen, they should create a database of facts; the database should have the following categorical headings: birth date and place, early-life activities (such as schooling, family involvement or lack of, formative experiences), personality traits, accomplishments, failures, friends, enemies, family, fears, desires, travels, discoveries, and place and time of death.

The database is crucial for effective research. It guides the students in their reading and enables them to focus on particulars that are not only important about the person they are researching but are also important for the creation of the script. Because the categories of the database provide students with a scaffold of what they need to look for as they are reading, the students will move more rapidly toward achieving mastery of their subject.

Once students have completed their databases, they should begin to construct their scripts.

Students should generate questions and answers for the actual person they have researched; they must also do the same for the two "guests" —pretenders—who are not telling the truth. As students create fictitious answers, they must do so in such a way that the answers sound true; in other words, the answers the two false guests give should not be too outrageous. As students work to fashion false answers, they must necessarily use both analytical and flexible thinking: analytical thinking to create answers that have the "ring" of truth; flexible thinking to create answers that are clever enough to possibly fool the audience. By creating the script, the students will be working more mindfully because they will know the purpose of their research (to inform, to entertain, and to "fool") and they will be reporting their findings in a new and novel way. Moreover, by selecting and synthesizing fact and fiction, students will have used higher level thinking (analysis, synthesis, evaluation).

Writing in Response to a Prompt: What Is a Hero?

Here's a typical writing prompt, one that might be found in the writing section of a standardized test:

> Heroic people come in all shapes and sizes. Some heroes, such as Superman and Wonder Woman, are famous. Other heroes, however, are not. But all heroes have some things in common: they are usually brave, they are usually determined, and they usually do things that help other people.
>
> Think of someone you know who is a hero. This person may be someone you know personally, someone you've seen, or someone you've read about.
>
> Create a paragraph about your hero. State what this person has done that is brave, determined, and selfless.

The key to responding to the prompt is to understand what it is asking you to do. To that end, you will need to be able to generate the right kind of content; convey it in the best form (i.e., a clearly structured paragraph); express the content in ways that satisfy appropriate purposes for a specific audience. The following procedures should be helpful:

Prewriting: Think and Identify

1. Note the heroic qualities in the prompt that you could use as controlling ideas in your paragraph: *brave* or *selfless*.

2. Think of people who have been brave, in word or deed, or have accomplished something unusual.

3. Choose one person.

4. Think about what this person has done or said that was brave, or what this person has accomplished that was unusual.

Writing: Constructing an Explanatory Paragraph

1. An explanatory paragraph has five parts:

   a. a topic sentence that states the idea the paragraph is going to develop

   b. a restriction (definition) sentence that limits the discussion

   c. an example of the idea in the topic sentence

   d. a discussion of how the example proves the idea in the topic sentence

   e. a concluding sentence that wraps up the paragraph

2. The paragraph must also have:

   a. clearly structured sentences that proceed logically from idea to idea

   b. sentence variety (including the opening sentence)

   c. concrete language that reflects strong voice (strong verbs and figurative language will help)

   d. clear transitions between sentences

Example One:

My Uncle J. is a hero. He is a brave person. He once got a lady's purse back from someone who took it. I think my Uncle J. is a hero.

Example Two:

To look at him, you wouldn't think my Uncle J. is a hero. He doesn't look like the typical heroes that you normally see in the movies. Even though he is only 5-feet-7-inches tall and is a little overweight, my Uncle J. is one of the bravest people I know. I discovered how brave he was when we were on vacation at South Padre Island last summer. We had gone to the beach to take a swim and had just put down our towels, lawn chairs, and cooler when we heard a scream. Suddenly we saw a guy racing our way; behind him was a woman flailing her arms and screaming that her purse had just been grabbed. I didn't know what to do, but my Uncle J. launched himself toward the guy, who was holding a purse like a football. In a matter of seconds, my Uncle threw himself at the guy. My Uncle tackled him with so much force that both he and the purse-grabber flew into the water. At that point, other people ran to help and pulled both my Uncle and the thief out of the water. By helping out the woman whose purse had been taken, my Uncle showed his heroic qualities. More important, though, my Uncle displayed bravery by tackling the thief in the water. You see, my Uncle doesn't know how to swim. What bravery he showed by putting someone else's welfare above his own safety!

Notice that example one contains only small, simple sentences. The verbs are weak (most are linking or nonspecific). There is no expansion of thought as conveyed through various phrases and clauses.

Example two, on the other hand, is much more developed. It contains a clear definition and a sequence of events that exemplify the definition. The sentences are varied and contain a rich mixture of phrases and clauses.

Reproducible Masters

Writing Activity: Nouns

Complete the following pattern with abstract and concrete nouns. In the first blank put an abstract noun; in the second blank put a concrete noun that tells something about the abstract noun.

I can't see _____,

but I can see _____.

I can't see love, but I can see a wedding ring.

I can't see chaos, but I can see a tornado.

I can't see happiness, but I can see a smile.

I can't hear anger, but I can hear a yelling.

I can't hear peace, but I can hear a silence.

I can't see joy, but I can see _____.

I can't hear sadness, but I can hear _____.

I can't hear victory, but I can hear _____.

I can't see innocence, but I can see _____.

I can't see peace, but I can see _____.

I can't see beauty, but I can see _____.

I can't see _____,

but I can see _____.

I can't hear _____,

but I can hear _____.

Writing Activity: Verbs—What Am I?

Think of a specific noun (animal or machine); think of four or five specific actions that the animal or machine does.

Use this pattern:

I _____, and I _____, and

I _____, and I _____.

What am I?

I leap, and I plop, and I swim, and I croak.
What am I? (A frog!)

I flit, and I fly, I flutter, and I fold my wings.
What am I? (A butterfly!)

Try your own:

_____

_____

Writing Activity: Three Verb Combinations

Think of an animal, object, or machine; think of three actions that the animal or machine does. Tell where the animal, object or machine does each action.

The mighty bullfrog swims through the pond, leaps to a lily pad, and croaks beneath the moon.

The comet soared through the skies, arced from star to star, and raced around the sun.

Try your own:

_____

_____

Writing Activity: *Adding Absolutes*

Add absolute phrases to the following sentences. For sentences one through four, add absolute phrases that describe (noun + participle); for sentences five through seven, add absolute phrases that show cause.

1. _____,

   the queen cackled.

2. _____,

   the giant bellowed.

3. _____,

   the hen squawked.

4. _____,

   the troll wept.

5. _____,

   the carriage stopped.

6. _____,

   the wolf growled.

7. _____,

   Cinderella danced.

Create your own sentences with absolute phrases. Describe a favorite person, character, animal, or thing. You might try describing a picture or photograph.

Writing Activity: *A Gerund Poem*

First, think of a book you have read, an event you have attended, or something else that has lots of people doing lots of things in the same place. Examples:

> fairy tales, a baseball stadium, a family gathering, an evening at the mall, etc.

Choose one place. Make a list of all the actions there. Describe those actions with gerund phrases. Example:

> A baseball stadium: Throwing fastballs, running bases, sliding home, calling strikes, hawking peanuts, watching fireworks, buying tickets, looking for seats, yelling at the umpire, seeing your team win, going home happy.

Second, begin with a statement like: A baseball stadium is . . . When you want to introduce a new set of actions, repeat the line.

Third, list gerund phrases after the opening statement. Example:

> Baseball is
> buying tickets, pushing through throngs of spectators, searching for seats, waving pennants, munching peanuts.
>
> Baseball is
> throwing fastballs, belting triples, running bases, sliding home.
>
> Baseball is
> yelling at the umpire, leaping into the "wave," holding your breath as a homerun barely clears the centerfield fence, watching fireworks burst overhead, pushing through the throng of baseball fans, going home happy.

Try your own gerund poem.

Writing Activity: An Infinitive Poem

First, think of characters from books you have read: Rumpelstiltskin, Rapunzel, Dorothy, Harry Potter, Hansel, etc.

Second, choose one character:

the wolf (from "The Three Pigs")

Third, think of five things the character wanted and five things the character did not want. Use the infinitive form: to . . .

wanted	did not want
to blow down houses	to go hungry
to play tricks	to build a house
to eat three pigs	to eat just one pig
to get into the brick house	to be foiled by brick walls
to dream of bacon sandwiches	to become wolf stew

Fourth, choose three or four infinitive phrases from each list. Use them in a poem. The first stanza might begin with the line: All I wanted was. . . . Begin the second stanza with the line: But I didn't want. . . .

All I wanted was

to blow down houses

to eat three pigs

to dream of bacon sandwiches.

But I didn't want

to build a house

to go hungry

to be foiled by brick walls

to become wolf stew.

Fifth, add adjectives to the phrases; change words; add additional phrases.

All I longed for was

> to blow down flimsy, pork-hiding houses,
>
> to lunch and munch on three plump pigs,
>
> to doze the day away and digest a delectable meal,
>
> to dream a delicious dream of succulent bacon sandwiches.

But I didn't want

> to labor, to sweat, to build a house of my own,
>
> to suffer the pangs of horrible hunger,
>
> to be foiled by a barrier of big brick walls,
>
> to slip down a chimney,
>
> to splash into a vat of water,
>
> to become wolf stew.

Try your own infinitive poem.

Writing Activity: *The Preposition Poem*

First, think of an animal, character, or object that is very active: a bird, a frog, an elf, a bouncing ball.

Second, choose one: a nightingale.

Third, choose five to ten prepositions (refer to the list of prepositions given in Chapter 1, Word Works VI); for example, in, on, below, above, beneath, through, beside, beyond, etc.

Fourth, write a poem in which you tell all the places your subject goes; use prepositional phrases. Begin with the line: The nightingale flew (tell where it went).

> The nightingale flew
>
> to the forest, through the trees,
>
> across the swamp, near an ogre,
>
> around the horn of a unicorn, toward a giant,
>
> between a pair of bats, beneath a bridge,
>
> away from a pair of elves, beyond the reach of a gremlin.

Fifth, add strong adjectives:

> The nightingale flew
>
> into the enchanted forest, through the thick tangle of trees,
>
> across the smoldering swamp, near a sleeping ogre,
>
> around the shiny horn of a unicorn, toward a grumpy giant,
>
> between a pair of gossiping bats, beneath the troll's battered bridge,
>
> away from a pair of acrobatic elves,
>
> beyond the reach of a gruesome gremlin, into the dusky twilight.

Try your own preposition poem.

Writing Activity: Adding Participles

Add two or three present participial phrases to the following sentences. Be sure to tell, with *-ing* phrases, what the subject of each sentence is doing. Examples:

1. _____, the giant fell asleep.

   Yawning widely, stretching his arms grotesquely, and sighing deeply, the giant fell asleep.

2. _____, the weaver's daughter wept.

   Eyeing the enormous size of her task and plopping herself down on the straw-strewn floor, the weaver's daughter wept.

3. _____, the wizened old man vanished.

   Whispering odd words under his breath and tapping his cane to the ground, the wizened old man vanished.

Now you try:

4. _____,
   the queen stepped into the room.

5. _____,
   the princess looked at her broken crown.

6. _____,
   Rapunzel ran to the window.

7. _____,
   the dwarf was a great cook.

8. The ogre, _____,
   stomped into the room.

9. The mean queen, _____,
   grabbed the magic mirror.

10. The elf, _____,
    couldn't believe his eyes.

Writing Activity: Adding Appositives

Add an appositive phrase to each of the following sentences.

Examples:

1. Achilles fought during the Trojan War.

    Achilles, *a powerful Greek warrior,* fought during the Trojan War.

    Achilles, *the Greek warrior with only one weak spot on his body,* fought during the Trojan War.

    Achilles, *the stalwart warrior who often sulked when he didn't get what he wanted,* fought during the Trojan War.

2. Hector was Achilles' enemy.

    Hector, *the breaker of horses,* was Achilles' enemy.

Now you try:

3. Rapunzel languished in her tower.

    _____

    _____

4. Cinderella loved glass shoes.

    _____

    _____

5. Snow White loved applesauce.

    _____

    _____

6. Gretel dropped bread crumbs in the forest.

    _____

    _____

Writing Activity: *A "Do You Remember When" Poem*

Imagine that you are telling a friend about all the adventures you had together. You can either write about yourself or about a character from something you have read.

Prewriting: Make a list of things you have done. The list can be real or "made up." Example:

one ogre talking to another ogre

played tricks on the elves

took the magician's magic hat

put electric eels in the castle moat

got caught in the dwarf's tunnel

scared the troll

almost got burned by the dragon

Drafting: Choose the best four items from your list; put them in a stanza. Begin with the line, "Do you remember when we . . ." Follow each line with a verb (past tense) phrase:

Do you remember when we

played tricks on the elves,

took the magician's magic hat,

put electric eels in the castle moat,

went into the cave?

Revising: Add more information to each of the four lines. Use strong nouns and verbs; add or get rid of words. Add phrases and clauses.

Do you remember when we

tricked the elves into thinking

we were Elvis come back to rock

from the Great Beyond?

Do you remember when we

swiped the magician's magic hat,

said the wrong spell, and

turned ourselves into wrangling rabbits?

Do you remember when we

dumped a bucket of baby electric eels

into the castle moat

the day the royal family went swimming?

Do you remember when we

crept into the cold cave

to cart off some coins and

almost got barbecued by the dragon?

- How is this revision different from the draft?
  What words have been changed?
  What phrases have been added?
  What clauses have been added?

- Words that have been changed: swiped (not took), dumped (not put), crept (not went)

- Prepositional phrases that have been added: from the Great Beyond, into wrangling rabbits, of baby electric eels, into the moat, into the cave, by the dragon

■ Infinitive phrases that have been added: to rock, to cart off some coins

■ Adverbial clauses that have been added: swiped the magician's magic hat, said the wrong spell, and turned ourselves into wrangling rabbits; crept into the cold cave, almost got barbecued

Editing/Sharing: Check to see that your revision has commas, periods, apostrophes, and question marks in the right places. Check to see that all the words are spelled correctly. Share the poem by reading it aloud.

Assessment Form

_____ The poem has at least one stanza comprised of questions recalling past adventures.

_____ Each question focuses on one activity.

_____ Each question contains concrete, specific language.

_____ Phrases and clauses are used effectively.

_____ The ideas and images in the poem fit together; they make sense together, and they work to support the main idea being expressed in the poem.

_____ Mechanical, spelling, and punctuation errors have been avoided.

Writing Activity: A "So Alone" Poem

Imagine that you are describing how it is to be alone. You can either write about yourself or about a character from something you have read.

Prewriting: Think of times when you were alone. Describe what you noticed (saw, heard, touched, tasted, smelled) and how you felt. You can also write from a character's point of view.
Example: Rapunzel

> a tower room, no way out, a table, a chair, a book, the old woman who visits her once a day, frustration, unhappiness

Drafting: Combine the items from step one in a poem. Describe where you are, what you notice, and how you feel (remember the idea is to tell what it is like to be lonely).

> I'm in a tower room
>
> there's no way out.
>
> It's lonely here.
>
> The only things here are
>
> a table, a chair,
>
> a book,
>
> and the old woman
>
> who visits me
>
> every day.

Revising: Add more information to each line. Use strong nouns and verbs; add or get rid of words. Avoid using abstract nouns. Add phrases and clauses.

I have no more numbers
for counting the days and nights
I have languished
in this tower room, this bolted box surrounded by sky,
that has neither ladder nor stairs.
My only company are
the table where I've scratched my initials,
the chair whose padding is flat
from so much sitting and waiting,
the book that I have read
so much that the ink has faded,
and the crone below
who makes me cringe and
whose cracked voice cackles
for me to let down my hair
again.

■ How is this revision different from the draft?
What words have been changed?
What phrases have been added?
What clauses have been added?

■ Words that have been changed: I have no more numbers for counting the days and nights I have languished in this tower room, this bolted box surrounded by sky, that has neither ladder, nor stairs (not "I'm in this tower room.").

■ Prepositional phrases that have been added: in this tower room, in the sky, from so much sitting, for me to let down my hair

■ Appositive phrase that has been added: this bolted box surrounded by sky

- Infinitive phrase that has been added: to let down my hair

- Adjective clauses that have been added: that has neither ladder, nor stairs; where I've scratched my initials, whose padding is flat, that I have read, who makes me cringe and whose cracked voice cackles

- Adverbial clause that has been added: that the ink has faded

Editing/Sharing: Check to see that your revision has commas, periods, apostrophes, and question marks in the right places. Check to see that all the words are spelled correctly. Share the poem by reading it aloud.

Assessment Form

_____ The poem has at least one stanza that describes the experience of being alone.

_____ The poem is filled with language that appeals to the senses: sight, sound, touch, smell, taste.

_____ The poem contains concrete, specific language.

_____ Phrases and clauses are used effectively.

_____ The ideas and images in the poem fit together; they make sense together, and they work to support the main idea being expressed in the poem.

_____ Mechanical, spelling, and punctuation errors have been avoided.

Works Cited

Blake, William. 1986. "The Tyger." In *Norton Anthology of English Literature*, 5th ed., vol. 2. General Ed. M. H. Abrams. New York: W.W. Norton & Co.

Burns, Robert. 1986. "A Red, Red Rose." In *Norton Anthology of English Literature*, 5th ed., vol. 2. General Ed. M. H. Abrams. New York: W.W. Norton & Co.

Calderonello, Alice, Virginia Martin, and Kritine Blair. 2003. *Grammar for Language Arts Teachers*. New York: Longman.

Good, Edward. 2002. *Whose Grammar Books Is This Anyway?* New York: MJF Books.

Haussamen, Brock, Amy Benjamin, Martha Kolln, and Rebecca Wheeler. 2003. *Grammar Alive! A Guide for Teachers*. Urbana, IL: NCTE.

Herrick, Robert. 2005. "The Argument of His Book." In *Norton Anthology of English Literature*, 8th ed., vol. 1. Ed. Stephen Greenblatt. New York: W.W. Norton & Co.

Hudson, Richard. 1992. *Teaching Grammar: A Guide for the National Curriculum*. Oxford, England: Blackwell.

Kolln, Martha. 1999. *Rhetorical Grammar: Grammatical Choices, Rhetorical Effects*. Boston: Allyn & Bacon.

Noden, Harry R. 1999. *Image Grammar*. Portsmouth, NH: Heinemann.

Noguchi, Rei R. 1991. *Grammar and the Teaching of Writing*. Urbana, IL: NCTE.

Pennington, Martha, Ed. 1995. *New Ways in Teaching Grammar*. Alexandria, VA: Teachers of English to Speakers of Other Languages.

Poe, Edgar Allen. 1990. "The Fall of the House of Usher." In *The American Tradition in Literature*, 7th ed. Ed. George Perkins, Scully Bradley, Richmond Croon Beatty, and E. Hudson Long. New York: McGraw-Hill.

Tennyson, Alfred Lord. 1986. "The Eagle." In *Norton Anthology of English Literature*, 5th ed., vol. 2. General Ed. M. H. Abrams. New York: W.W. Norton & Co.

Thurman, Susan. 2002. *The Everything Grammar and Style Book*. Avon, MA: Adams.

Weaver, Constance. 1996. *Teaching Grammar in Context*. Portsmouth, NH: Boynton/Cook, Heinemann.

Whitman, Walt. 1990. "The Song of Myself." In *The American Tradition in Literature*, 7th ed. Eds. George Perkins, Scully Bradley, Richmond Croon Beatty, and E. Hudson Long. New York: McGraw-Hill.

Wordsworth, William. 1986. "I Wandered Lonely as a Cloud." In *Norton Anthology of English Literature*, 5th ed., vol. 2. General Ed. M. H. Abrams. New York: W.W. Norton & Co.